The New Modern Poetry

British and American Poetry

Since World War II

The New Modern Poetry

British and American Poetry

Since World War II

Edited by M. L. Rosenthal

The Macmillan Company, New York

15860

Library of Congress Catalog Card Number: 66–17902

Fourth Printing 1968
The Macmillan Company, New York
Printed in the United States of America

ACKNOWLEDGMENTS

Acknowledgment is gratefully given to the following poets, their representatives, and publishers for permission to include the poems in this anthology:

GEORGE ALLEN & UNWIN LTD. for Austin Clarke's "Ancient Lights," "Respectable People" and "The Envy of Poor Lovers" from *Ancient Lights*, 1955; and "Intercessors" from *The Horse-Eaters*, 1960, all as reprinted in *Later Poems*, 1961.

A. ALVAREZ for his poems "Lost" and "Operation."

ATHENEUM PUBLISHERS for "Homage to the Weather," "Security" and "Omens" from *Weather and Season* by Michael Hamburger, copyright © 1963 by Michael Hamburger, and for "Woman at the Washington Zoo" by Randall Jarrell, from *Woman at the Washington Zoo* by Randall Jarrell, copyright © 1960 by Randall Jarrell.

JOHN BERRYMAN for "New Year's Eve" from *The Dispossessed*, Sloane, 1948.

PAUL BLACKBURN for "Good Morning Love!," "Song of the Hesitations" and "The Watchers."

ROBERT BLY for "Poem Against the Rich" and "Snowfall in the Afternoon" from *Silence in the Snowy Fields*, Wesleyan University Press, 1962.

CHATTO & WINDUS for "Furnished Lives" from *The Two Freedoms*, 1958, by Jon Silkin.

CHILMARK PRESS for "Sailing to an Island," "Girl at the Seaside" and "The Poet on the Island" by Richard Murphy, copyright 1963 by Richard Murphy.

CHRISTY & MOORE, LTD. for Dannie Abse's "The Second Coming" from *Tenants of the House*, 1957, and "After the Release of Ezra Pound" from *Poems Golders Green*, 1962.

1960 by Paul Goodman; "Long Lines" copyright © 1957 by Paul Goodman; and "April 1962," copyright © 1962 by Paul Goodman; for "If It Offend Thee . . ." from *Medusa in Gramercy Park* by Horace Gregory, copyright © 1958 by Horace Gregory; for "The Clown: He Dances in the Clearing by Night," "Postlude: for Goya" and "To and on Other Intellectual Poets on Reading That the U.S.A.F. Had Sent a Team of Scientists to Africa to Learn Why Giraffes Do Not Black Out" from *Graffiti* by Ramon Guthrie, copyright © 1959 by Ramon Guthrie; for "Drinking Song" from *A Summoning of Stones* by Anthony Hecht, copyright © 1954 by Anthony Hecht; for "Nuit Blanche" from *Out in the Open* by Katherine Hoskins, copyright © 1958 by Katherine Hoskins; for the following selections from *Poems from a Cage* by Dilys Laing: "Aubade," copyright © 1958 by Alexander Laing, and "Villanelle," copyright © 1961 by Alexander Laing; for "The Spanish War," "British Leftish Poetry," "Reflections in a Slum" and "Old Wife in High Spirits" from *Collected Poems* by Hugh MacDiarmid, copyright © 1962 by Christopher Murray Grieve; for "A Sky of Late Summer," copyright © 1965 by Henry Rago, and "Promise Your Hand," copyright © 1960 by Henry Rago from *A Sky of Late Summer* by Henry Rago; for "Beads from Blackpool," "Venetian Scene" and "Making Love, Killing Time" from *Selected Poems* by Anne Ridler, copyright 1951 by Anne Ridler; for the following selections from *Collected Poems 1937–1962* by Winfield Townley Scott: "The U.S. Sailor with the Japanese Skull" and "Into the Wind," copyright 1949, 1950, 1951, 1952, 1953, 1954, 1955, 1956, 1957, 1958, by Winfield Townley Scott; and "Three American Women and a German Bayonet," copyright 1946 by Winfield Townley Scott; for "Preface" from *Outlanders* by Theodore Weiss, copyright © 1952 by Theodore Weiss, "The Reapings" and "In the Round" from *The Medium*, copyright © 1965; and for "On the Suicide of a Friend," and "The Self and the Weather" from *The Self-Made Man* by Reed Whittemore, copyright © 1959 by Reed Whittemore.
THE MARVELL PRESS for "Dry-Point," "Myxomatosis," "Toads," "Poetry of Departures" and "Deceptions" by Philip Larkin from *The Less Deceived*, 1955.
CHRISTOPHER MIDDLETON for his poem "The Ancestors," which appeared in *Orient/West*, Vol. 8, No. 4, 1963.
JOHN MONTAGUE for his poems "Murphy in Manchester," "The First Invasion of Ireland" and "Poisoned Lands" from *Poisoned Lands and Other Poems*, 1961, and for "The Trout."
WILLIAM MORROW AND COMPANY, INC. for "An Aftermath," from *A Smell of Burning* by Thomas Blackburn, copyright © 1961 by Thomas Blackburn.
JOHN MURRAY LTD. for John Betjeman's "The Licorice Fields at Pontefract" and "Late-Flowering Lust" from *Collected Poems*, 1958.
HOWARD NEMEROV for his poems "The Scales of the Eyes" and "The Goose Fish" from *New and Selected Poems*, 1960; and "Lot Later" from *The Next Room of the Dream*, 1962.
NEW DIRECTIONS for "In Goya's Greatest Scenes" and "Away above a Harborful" from *A Coney Island of the Mind* by Lawrence Ferlinghetti, copyright © 1955, 1958 by Lawrence Ferlinghetti; for "Crystal Night" from "During the Eichmann Trial" from *The Jacob's Ladder* by Denise Levertov, copyright © 1961 by Denise Levertov Goodman; for "A Sword in a Cloud of Light" from *Natural Numbers* by Kenneth Rexroth, copyright 1940, 1963 by Kenneth Rexroth; and for "Starlight Like Intuition Pierced the Twelve" from *Vaudeville for a Princess* by Delmore Schwartz, copyright © 1950 by New Directions.
HAROLD OBER ASSOCIATES for "Bucolic," copyright © 1960 by W. S. Merwin, and "Fog-Horn," copyright © 1958 by W. S. Merwin from *The Drunk in the Furnace* by W. S. Merwin, published by The Macmillan Company, 1964; "Fog-Horn" originally appeared in *The New Yorker*.

TO MY SON DAVID

Contents

(x v)

Introduction

I should have liked to make an astringent anthology, with no poem but rode brilliantly on the brimming page like Yeats's wild swans on the water, or cracked cleanly and violently through the gross twentieth-century air, or laughed as purely as the gods summoned to see Aphrodite and Ares in Hephaestus's net. As Hugh MacDiarmid says, "the kind of poetry I want" is

> A speech, a poetry, to bring to bear upon life
> The concentrated strength of all our being. . . .

Do we have such poetry in our age, the age of the score of years since World War II? Yes, if we limit ourselves to the very best work of a very few figures. We shall have very little Homeric laughter though plenty of grimmer or hysterical laughter. But we shall have much beauty of a fine and special sort, not free of agony but derived from it and bearing it along, as it were, in flight.

To certain temperaments, the most sensitive if not necessarily the most "healthy-minded," the pressures and violence of two centuries seem to have grown too intense for personality to cope with in the old sense. For this reason, much of our most impressive poetry of the earlier part of the century—*The Waste Land*, the *Cantos, The Bridge*—sought directly through art for means of redefining and reconstructing the exposed and blasted Self. The program is a romantic one, and indeed the beginnings of this development do lie in the backgrounds and struggles of the great Romantic poets. But it is in the triumph of a nonhumanist technology, of abstract, impersonal, mechanical force in the real world, that the *horror* lies whose fullest expression is modern war and the nuclear bomb. The issues are so obvious that we tend to overlook their pervasive presence in all our art, but their disintegrating effect on poetic form and sensibility is inescapable. Their pressure is such that we need not seek it merely in the overt statement of them, though plenty of poems do state them plainly enough. It is evident in such phenomena as the absolute self-exposure of certain recent poets, the breakdown of distinctions between the tragic and the comic (resulting in a considerable buffoonery of naked clowning), the presence of a heavy atmosphere of depression, and the diversion of expectations of aesthetic structure in a writer like

Robert Duncan. (Such a writer goes beyond the surface violations of conventional form of someone like Cummings. He wilfully interferes with the inner organic form, however "free," of his own poems, in his effort to give first place in the making of a poem to the process of making itself.)

These tendencies are the most forceful ones of the period following hard upon the last war. However, I have sought to suggest not only these major directions, though they interest me most, but the whole range of American and British, including Irish, poetry during this period. If I have given a certain emphasis to the strongest figures, I fight no wars here against the others who with honor, verve, and dedication have dared to write under banners of their own or no banners at all. One poet has a genius for serene, visionary rapture, let the fallout drop as it may (not that he's unconcerned about that question as a man, either). Another has the quick, caricaturing eye and ear for the world as it is that are almost better than thought or feeling. Another's gift is purely lyrical, or purely elegiac. The finely subtle poets, the very quiet yet very true ones, and those whose sense of discrimination controls them so exquisitely that they would never dream of doing an easy thing or a thing already done by anyone else are the poets most likely to be neglected by all of us. "I can love both fair and brown" —and so, for the sake of poetry and the race, I hope we all can. I have reviewed as much of the poetry since the war as leisure, knowledge, and access have permitted, and have selected from it a widely representative spectrum. Though all anthologies are unjust, I have at least not *voted* for injustice.

I have tried, that is, to read the poetry with love, and to select poems of a sufficient relevance and quality, poems that *tell* in their own way somehow, hoping that the group thus arrived at will have its own lessons to teach us, apart from our preconceptions. The first result of this effort has perhaps been a certain liberation from the dominance of recent anthologies that have emphasized the work of the youngest writers only, or of special groups or tendencies only. These anthologies have their valid uses as manifestoes, mutual assistance pacts, or joint displays of new or unknown talent. Coteries are not usually dishonest or self-seeking, but reflect genuine conviction and the influence of strong personalities. Let us, then, pay attention to their genuine accomplishments (each contains at least one pearl for every dozen oysters, say) without letting them blind us to the presence of other styles, other meanings.

One must remember, for instance, that a number of the outstanding poets of the past twenty years—I do not refer to grand old monuments of a bygone age, but to people who have given us something with new life in it since the war—have been neither youngsters nor members of the new "schools." They are neither "confessional" poets, nor "Beats," nor "Sixties" poets in this country, nor adherents of the "Group" or the "Movement" or one of the national groupings in the British Isles. Originally, indeed, I hoped to represent the postwar work of such elder figures of continuing significance as Williams, Frost, Stevens, and Pound. Problems of space and, especially, of permissions costs have made this aim of putting their work side by side with that of the younger people impracticable. Instead, I must simply remind the reader that all these writers, and some of their other contemporaries, continued to develop for varying periods after the war. Equally important, they stand as reminders to the young that ultimately the real competition is with the qualitative realizations and difficult craft of the masters.

I have not, however, been thoroughly consistent in omitting the elder masters. The figures named, and certain younger ones such as Auden, Spender, and MacNeice, are so well known that including them here would be of no special service to American readers. On the other hand, the germinative work of the Scottish poet Hugh MacDiarmid (Christopher Grieve) has yet to receive proper recognition in this country, and even Edwin Muir remains too little known. The important Irish poet Austin Clarke is even less well known. As with the young "unknowns," I have made my choices in terms of what my sense of the whole poetic situation leads me to think will be especially useful or informative or meaningful to interested American readers at this time. I refer, of course, to the poetic situation of the past two decades; "modern poetry" has taken on a new cast, has new centers of interest now. This book, then, is decisively of this time despite the varied ages of the poets represented. It contains virtually nothing published in book form before 1945; the only exceptions are one or two war poems of significance that appeared no earlier than 1943. I have wished to stress the *phenomenon* of the coexistence of different generations genuinely engaged in the living stream of their art, rather than to call undue attention to any particular poet's age.

It might have been wise to keep American and British poets divided, and perhaps to include subsections of Irish, Scottish, and even Canadian poets (for a few of these too have crept into this book, so unguarded are our cultural borders these days). But I am simply not sure that this division would be as useful or interesting as superficially it might seem to be. For better or for worse, we do have an international poetry of the English language now, in some important sense at any rate. Robert Lowell and Ted Hughes are patently closer to one another than the former is, for instance, to Robert Bly or the latter to Charles Causley. It is useful to think of Howard Nemerov, Charles Tomlinson, and Thomas Kinsella as related to one another in certain qualities of keenness and openness to the international currents of sensibility; and of Paul Goodman and Kenneth Rexroth as comparable with D. J. Enright and Edwin Brock, not so much in the ultimate poetic note or ability as in the kind of sense of life, at once political and private, they are after. Admittedly, there are different national tones and preoccupations. Particularly, the Americans are much the most likely to go to extremes of form and passionate statement. And from another viewpoint, figures like Allen Ginsberg, Patrick Kavanagh, and R. S. Thomas seem very local in, respectively, their second-generation American, transplanted rural Irish, and rural Welsh orientation. Yet all have become international property as well. Sophisticated writers like Michael Hamburger and Christopher Middleton in England or Theodore Weiss and Randall Jarrell in our country take an international orientation for granted, often with a Continental base of reference. Again, an articulate, intensely nervous, rapid-fire assimilator of concrete detail like the English Peter Redgrove seems to an American to be talking a recognizable language, while (an old story) it was to England that the young and now tragically dead Sylvia Plath went to find her true way as a poet.

Putting the poets together without regard to nationality does not diminish their unavoidably national qualities. The local detail, flavor, and sense of history come through in the very language of most of these poems, quite as much as in their literal subject matter. These will be mostly self-evident, I believe. But the happily neutral use of alphabetical rather than national arrangement gives the poems fuller play in their own right than they would otherwise have. The great differences, really, are less between countries than between cosmopolitan and provincial awareness, or between the poetry of anguished identification of the inner self with the state of the culture and the poetry of cool objectivity, or between the poets who experiment with rhythms and with form generally and those who find conventional forms congenial to their effort, however individual their thought and language may be.

Looking for a moment at the beginning of my table of contents, let me make some notes on the kind of facts that emerge.

The accident of alphabetical order makes Dannie Abse's "The Second Coming" our opening poem, its theme the destructive effect of the machine on the mythopoeic instinct of man. The next poem, again by Dr. Abse, concerns the meaning of Ezra Pound's career, that prize puzzle of the age—the relationship of art and morality. Two poems by A. Alvarez, England's chief critical advocate of "American" violence and extremism in poetry, take us into the brutal sense of the modern dependence on a personal ethic without regard to any relationship but purely personal ones. Kingsley Amis's witty confusions, the humbled self-castigation of Brother Antoninus, the ulcerous wryness of John Berryman, all betray a certain uncompromising candor in so many different modes. So, oddly, do the popular poems of John Betjeman here included—the first self-ironic, the second almost morbidly truthful. Paul Blackburn's "The Watchers" (skipping past other names and titles) is a technically original poem, its balances and sound relationships worked out with the help of the tape recorder, clearly in the Poundian tradition but directed to a sense of actual reality rather than of the grand perspectives of Dantean tradition. Add a romantically rich dimension and a certain bitter yet idealistic turn to the sort of thing "The Watchers" does, and the connection, a bit further on, with Robert Duncan's work seems clear. But Paul Blackburn's deliberately unheroic and familiar language in his other poems here is an important indication of the rise of a new tendency to employ the common idiom in poetry. The aim now seems less that of finding a democratic medium and a folk-directness than of bringing the casual immediacy of experience directly into the shape of poems. The casual, the unpretentious, the supposedly incidental—what used to be called the "antipoetic," but less belligerently deployed now—these define the surface of a good deal of current poetry. Together with Paul Blackburn, Robert Creeley, Denise Levertov, Lawrence Ferlinghetti, and Ian Hamilton Finlay are possibly the outstanding, if inconsistent, practitioners here represented of this mode. But it colors the work of many others to some extent. One might say that the British style of journalistic poetry that comments on events in the news, on political problems, and on social ironies (Thwaite, Wain) is, though more rhetorical and though poetically not as seriously conceived, related in character—a poetry deliberately stripped of pretension at the risk of betraying the poetic tradition itself. An American figure like Reed Whittemore, whose poetry does not sink itself into the existential moment as Paul Blackburn's at its best does, nevertheless deliberately reduces the emotional charge of his work with apparently the same purpose of getting out from under the burden both of tradition and of aesthetic responsibility at once.

These men and women write out of their individual natures, of course. No general formula will cover the whole picture. But when their work, in its varied fashions, reaches what for each is his highest possibility, it takes on something of a bitterly intense and essentially despairing consciousness. The "withdrawal" of the casual, self-discounting, emotion-evading poets is but another facet of the terror that the greatest figures deal with head-on. The memories of the last war, with its genocide and mass bombings and finally the Bomb, have branded themselves deep within the psyche of this age. Much of the poetry criticizes the prevailing order of things with a sort of helpless severity. Much of it mocks the order or is fascinated by private ugliness and violence. Much of it expresses the sense of a precarious moment in time, with pain at the memory of values and solid dependabilities already crumbled away and at the expectation that soon much more will be lost. (Here the Irish poets, the English, and the Americans are totally at one.) And yet is it not true that our writers can be lighthearted, lyrical, and loving as well, proving that man and, thank God, woman are still what they always were? Yes, naturally—yet if there was ever a body of work suggesting heroism, and even sometimes gaiety, on a burning ship surely this must be it.

Technically, it seems clear, the bold advances of the earlier part of the century in the wake of the French Symbolists, the development of the poetic sequence as the chief form of the longer poem, the experimentation with formal modes that would allow greater functional flexibility while exploiting many traditional echoes, and the renewal of a dramatically alive poetic rhetoric have not been surpassed in our two decades. Rediscoveries keep being made, such as the minor one by Robert Bly and James Wright of the possibility of using surrealist vision in a very simple kind of poetry, or the extensions by Charles Olson and Robert Duncan of improvisational montage or collage techniques borrowed from Pound and Williams (with some possible advances by Duncan especially), or—most significantly—by Lowell of the principle of breakneck speed in the piling up of images, emotional accumulation, and shifts of points of focus. Our poets, in this country primarily, have been turning to European poetry once again, after a long period of absorption of methods at least a generation old, to learn how to unlock their energies in slightly unfamiliar ways. I have rigorously, and regretfully, excluded translations from this collection in the interest of presenting primary work only, but there is no doubt a new germinative process under way under the influence of such figures as Montale, Pasternak, and various others neglected by us while so long under the spell almost exclusively of the French. In this whole matter of form, it is only a few masters, ever, who advance the range of an art by devising techniques to meet the pressures of sensibility. Ordinarily, such masters arise one or two at a time and are recognized, not by their external techniques but by the absolute authority of their language and of the way their poems move into decisive definition.

M. L. ROSENTHAL

Suffern, N. Y.
February, 1965

The New Modern Poetry

British and American Poetry

Since World War II

DANNIE ABSE

The Second Coming

The ground twitches and the noble head
(so often painted) breaks through the cracked crust,
hair first, then ivory forehead into the sunlit field;
the earth yields silently to the straining.
A blackbird flies away.

  The eyes open suddenly
just above the grass, seeing corn. No man is near.
Sound of days of heat, of silence.
It is lonely to be born.
And now He's breathing—air not earth
who inhaled worms and death so long.

Still His body in darkness, lightward pushing.
Pause, rest, He is tired now, enough to delight
in looking. Is this true: the world all heaven,
head in corn, with pale butterflies
staggering over Him?

  He cannot rise further.
The earth is heavy on His shoulders.
Cry out, shout, oh help is near.
Dangerously, the machine passes scything corn,
but the driver does not hear, cannot hear
—and now that noble head is gone,
a liquid redness in the yellow
where the mouth had been.

Dig, I say dig, you'll
find arms, loins, white legs, to prove my story—
and one red poppy in the corn.

After the Release of Ezra Pound

"In Jerusalem I asked
the ancient Hebrew poets to forgive you,
and what would Walt Whitman have said
and Thomas Jefferson?"
                    —PAUL POTTS

In Soho's square mile of unoriginal sin
where the fraudulent neon lights haunt,
but cannot hide, the dinginess of vice,
the jeans and sweater boys spoke of Pound,
and you, Paul, repeated your question.

The chee-chee bums in Torino's laughed and
the virgins of St. Martin's School of Art.
The corner spivs with their Maltese masks
loitered for the two o'clock result,
and those in the restaurants of Greek Street
eating income tax did not hear the laugh.

Gentle Gentile, you asked the question.
Free now (and we praise this) Pound could answer.

The strip lighting of Soho did not fuse,
no blood trickled from a certain book
down the immaculate shelves of Zwemmer's.
But the circumcized did not laugh.
The swart nudes in the backrooms put on clothes
and the doors of the French pub closed.

Pound did not hear the raw Jewish cry,
the populations committed to the dark
when he muttered through microphones
of murderers. He, not I, must answer.

Because of the structures of a beautiful poet
you ask the man who is less than beautiful,
and wait in the public neurosis of Soho,
in the liberty of loneliness for an answer.

(2)

In the beer and espresso bars they talked
of Ezra Pound, excusing the silences of an old man,
saying there is so little time between
the parquet floors of an institution
and the boredom of the final box.

Why, Paul, if that ticking distance between
was merely a journey long enough
to walk the circumference of a Belsen,
Walt Whitman would have been eloquent,
and Thomas Jefferson would have cursed.

A. ALVAREZ

Lost

My sleep falters and the good dreams:
The sky lit green, you reaching, reaching out
Through a bell of air. I stir.

The same wrist lies along my cheek;
My fingers touch it. The same head on my chest
Stirs. My arms round the same body;
And I feel the dead arms stir.
My fingers in the same dead hair.
The same belly, dead thighs stir.

The dream whirrs, cuts. The day blinks, stirs.
Hers. Not yours, my love. Hers.

Operation

The town froze, close as a fist.
Winter was setting about us.
Like birds the bare trees shivered,

(3)

Birds without leaves or nests
As the fog took over.

My words were all gone, my tongue sour.
We sat in the car like the dead
Awaiting the dead. Your hair
Wept round your face like a willow
Unstirring. Your eyes were dry.

Unbodied, like smoke in the crowd,
You vanished. Later came violence.
Not that you felt it or cared,
Swaddled in drugs, apart
In some fractured, offensive dream,
While a bog-Irish nurse mopped up.

"Leave me. I'm bleeding. I bleed
Still. But he didn't hurt me."
Pale as the dead. As the dead
Fragile. Vague as the city
Now the fog chokes down again.
A life was pitched out like garbage.

"I bleed still. A boy, they said."
My blood stings like a river
Lurching over the falls.
My hands are bloody. My mind
Is rinsed with it. Blood fails me.
You lie like the dead, still bleeding,
While his fingers, unformed, unerring,
Hold us and pick us to pieces.

A Dream of Fair Women

The door still swinging to, and girls revive,
Aeronauts in the upmost altitudes
    Of boredom fainting, dive
Into the bright oxygen of my nod;
Angels as well, a squadron of draped nudes,
    They rear towards their god.

Militant all, they fight to take my hat,
No more as yet; the other men retire
    Insulted, gestured at;
Each girl presses on me her share of what
Makes up the barn-door target of desire:
    And I am a crack shot.

Speech fails them, amorous, but each one's look,
Endorsed in other ways, begs me to sign
    Her body's autograph-book;
"Me first, Kingsley; I'm cleverest" each declares,
But no gourmet races downstairs to dine,
    Nor will I race upstairs.

Feigning aplomb, perhaps for half an hour,
I hover, and am shown by each princess
    The entrance to her tower;
Open, in that its tenant throws the key
At once to anyone, but not unless
    That anyone is me.

Now from the corridor their fathers cheer,
Their brothers, their young men; the cheers increase
    As soon as I appear;
From each I win a handshake and sincere
Congratulations; from the chief of police
    A nod, a wink, a leer.

This over, all delay is over too;
The first eight girls (the roster now agreed)
    Leap on me, and undo . . .
But honesty impels me to confess
That this is "all a dream," which was, indeed,
    Not difficult to guess.

But wait; not "just a dream," because, though good
And beautiful, it is also true, and hence
    Is rarely understood;
Who would choose any feasible ideal
In here and now's giant circumference,
    If that small room were real?

Only the best; the others find, have found
Love's ordinary distances too great,
    And, eager, stand their ground;
Map-drunk explorers, dry-land sailors, they
See no arrival that can compensate
    For boredom on the way;

And, seeming doctrinaire, but really weak,
Limelighted dolls guttering in their brain,
    They come with me, to seek
The halls of theoretical delight,
The women of that ever-fresh terrain,
    The night after to-night.

I Am Long Weaned

"When I looked for good then evil came, and
when I waited for light then came darkness.
My bowels boil, and rest not."
—*The Book of Job*

I am long weaned.

My mouth, puckered on gall,
Sucks dry curd.

My thoughts, those sterile watercourses
Scarring a desert.

My throat is lean meat.
In my belly no substance is,
Nor water moves.

My gut goes down
A straight drop to my groin.

My cod is withered string,
My seed, two flints in a sack.

Some day, in some other place,
Will come a rain;
Will come water out of deep wells,
Will come melons sweet from the vine.

I will know God.

Sophia, deep wisdom,
The splendid unquenchable fount:

Unbind those breasts.

New Year's Eve

The grey girl who had not been singing stopped,
And a brave new no-sound blew through acrid air.
I set my drink down, hard. Somebody slapped
Somebody's second wife somewhere,
Wheeling away to long to be alone.
I see the dragon of years is almost done,
Its claws loosen, its eyes
Crust now with tears & lust and a scale of lies.

A whiskey-listless and excessive saint
Was expounding his position, whom I hung
Boy-glad in glowing heaven: he grows faint:
Hearing what song the sirens sung,
Sidelong he web-slid and some rich prose spun.
The tissue golden of the gifts undone
Surpassed the gifts. Miss Weirs
Whispers to me her international fears.

Intelligentsia milling. In a semi-German
(Our loss of Latin fractured how far our fate,—
Disinterested once, linkage once like a sermon)
I struggle to articulate
Why it is our promise breaks in pieces early.
The Muses' visitants come soon, go surly
With liquor & mirrors away
In this land wealthy & casual as a holiday.

Whom the Bitch winks at. Most of us are linsey-
woolsey workmen, grandiose, and slack.
On m'analyse, the key to secrets. Kinsey
Shortly will tell us sharply back
Habits we stuttered. How revive to join
(Great evils grieve beneath: eye Caesar's coin)
And lure a while more home
The vivid wanderers, uneasy with our shame?

Priests of the infinite! ah, not for long.
The dove whispers, and diminishes
Up the blue leagues. And no doubt we heard wrong—
Wax of our lives collects & dulls; but was
What we heard hurried as we memorized,
Or brightened, or adjusted? Undisguised
We pray our tongues & fingers
Record the strange word that blows suddenly and lingers.

Imagine a patience in the works of love
Luck sometimes visits. Ages we have sighed,
And cleave more sternly to a music of
Even this sore word "genocide."
Each to his own! Clockless & thankless dream
And labour Makers, being what we seem.
Soon soon enough we turn
Our tools in; brownshirt Time chiefly our works will burn.

I remember: white fine flour everywhere whirled
Ceaselessly, wheels rolled, a slow thunder boomed,
And there were snowy men in the mill-world
With sparkling eyes, light hair uncombed,
And one of them was humming an old song,
Sack upon sack grew portly, until strong
Arms moved them on, by pairs,
And then the bell clanged and they ran like hares.

Scotch in his oxter, my Retarded One
Blows in before the midnight; freezing slush
Stamps off, off. Worst of years! . . . no matter, begone;
Your slash and spells (in the sudden hush)
We see now we had to suffer some day, so
I cross the dragon with a blessing, low,
While the black blood slows. Clock-wise,
We clasp upon the stroke, kissing with happy cries.

Dream Song 29

There sat down, once, a thing on Henry's heart
só heavy, if he had a hundred years
& more, & weeping, sleepless, in all them time
Henry could not make good.
Starts again always in Henry's ears
the little cough somewhere, an odour, a chime.

And there is another thing he has in mind
like a grave Sienese face a thousand years
would fail to blur the still profiled reproach of. Ghastly,
with open eyes, he attends, blind.
All the bells say: too late. This is not for tears;
thinking.

But never did Henry, as he thought he did,
end anyone and hacks her body up
and hide the pieces, where they may be found.
He knows: he went over everyone, & nobody's missing.
Often he reckons, in the dawn, them up.
Nobody is ever missing.

JOHN BETJEMAN

The Licorice Fields at Pontefract

In the licorice fields at Pontefract
   My love and I did meet
And many a burdened licorice bush
   Was blooming round our feet;
Red hair she had and golden skin,
Her sulky lips were shaped for sin,
Her sturdy legs were flannel-slack'd,
The strongest legs in Pontefract.

(1 0)

The light and dangling licorice flowers
    Gave off the sweetest smells;
From various black Victorian towers
    The Sunday evening bells
Came pealing over dales and hills
And tanneries and silent mills
And lowly streets where county stops
And little shuttered corner shops.

She cast her blazing eyes on me
    And plucked a licorice leaf;
I was her captive slave and she
    My red-haired robber chief.
Oh love! for love I could not speak,
It left me winded, wilting, weak
And held in brown arms strong and bare
And wound with flaming ropes of hair.

Late-Flowering Lust

My head is bald, my breath is bad,
    Unshaven is my chin,
I have not now the joys I had
    When I was young in sin.

I run my fingers down your dress
    With brandy-certain aim
And you respond to my caress
    And maybe feel the same.

But I've a picture of my own
    On this reunion night,
Wherein two skeletons are shewn
    To hold each other tight;

Dark sockets look on emptiness
    Which once was loving-eyed,
The mouth that opens for a kiss
    Has got no tongue inside.

(1 1)

I cling to you inflamed with fear
    As now you cling to me,
I feel how frail you are my dear
    And wonder what will be—

A week? or twenty years remain?
    And then—what kind of death?
A losing fight with frightful pain
    Or a gasping fight for breath?

Too long we let our bodies cling,
    We cannot hide disgust
At all the thoughts that in us spring
    From this late-flowering lust.

ELIZABETH   BISHOP

Faustina, or Rock Roses

Tended by Faustina
yes in a crazy house
upon a crazy bed,
frail, of chipped enamel,
blooming above her head
into four vaguely rose-like
    flower-formations,

the white woman whispers to
herself. The floorboards sag
this way and that. The crooked
towel-covered table
bears a can of talcum
and five pasteboard boxes
    of little pills,

most half-crystallized.
The visitor sits and watches
the dew glint on the screen
and in it two glow-worms
burning a drowned green.
Meanwhile the eighty-watt bulb
   betrays us all,

discovering the concern
within our stupefaction;
lighting as well on heads
of tacks in the wall paper,
on a paper wall-pocket,
violet-embossed, glistening
   with mica-flakes.

It exposes the fine white hair,
the gown with the undershirt
showing at the neck,
the pallid palm-leaf fan
she holds but cannot wield
her white disordered sheets
   like wilted roses.

Clutter of trophies,
chamber of bleached flags!
—Rags or ragged garments
hung on the chairs and hooks
each contributing its
shade of white, confusing
   as undazzling.

The visitor is embarrassed
not by pain nor age
nor even nakedness,
though perhaps by its reverse.
By and by the whisper
says, *"Faustina, Faustina . . ."*
   "¡Vengo, señora!"

(*1 3*)

On bare scraping feet
Faustina nears the bed.
She exhibits the talcum powder,
the pills, the cans of "cream,"
the white bowl of farina,
requesting for herself
    a little *coñac*;

complaining of, explaining,
the terms of her employment.
She bends above the other.
Her sinister kind face
presents a cruel black
coincident conundrum.
    Oh, is it

freedom at last, a lifelong
dream of time and silence,
dream of protection and rest?
Or is it the very worst,
the unimaginable nightmare
that never before dared last
    more than a second?

The acuteness of the question
forks instantly and starts
a snake-tongue flickering;
blurs further, blunts, softens,
separates, falls, our problems
becoming helplessly
proliferative.

There is no way of telling.
The eyes say only either.
At last the visitor rises,
awkwardly proffers her bunch
of rust-perforated roses
and wonders oh, whence come
    all the petals.

(1 4)

While Someone Telephones

Wasted, wasted minutes that couldn't be worse,
minutes of a barbaric condescension.
—Stare out the bathroom window at the fir-trees,
at their dark needles, accretions to no purpose
woodenly crystallized, and where two fireflies
are only lost.
Hear nothing but a train that goes by, must go by, like tension;
nothing. And wait:
maybe even now these minutes' host
emerges, some relaxed uncondescending stranger,
the heart's release.
And while the fireflies
are failing to illuminate these nightmare trees
might they not be his green gay eyes.

PAUL   BLACKBURN

Good Morning Love!

Rise at 7:15
study the
artifacts
          (2 books
           1 photo
           1 gouache sketch
           2 unclean socks
perform the neces-
sary ablutions
          hands
          face
          feet
          crotch)

(1 5)

even answer the door with good grace, even
if it's the light & gas man
announcing himself as "EDISON!
Readjer meter mister?"
For Christ sake yes
read my meter
Nothing can alter the euphoria
The blister is still on one finger
             There just are
some mornings worth getting up
             & making a cup
of coffee that's all

Song of the Hesitations

The moon is setting in the west
the hour near four o'clock
Temperature's down, wind is high
I'm walking toward the docks

Loose sheets of old newspapers whirl
above my head like gulls
are circling above the subway grates
are diving for the kill—

where I'm the fish in the empty street
that's caught below the wind
One newsprint bird tears at my cheek
another swoops behind

and wraps its rattling wings about
my frozen face with love
I read a headline on one wing
VISIONS THAT LED TO DEATH

And I *will* sing of Death and Love
But still I am not drunk enough
to dream us into Spring

The Watchers

It's going to rain
Across the avenue a crane
whose name is
         CIVETTA LINK-BELT
dips, rises and turns in a
    graceless geometry

    But grace is slowness   /   as
ecstasy is some kind of speed or madness   /
The crane moves slowly, that
much it is graceful   /   The men
    watch and the leaves

Cranes make letters in the sky
    as the wedge flies
        The scholar's function is

            Mercury, thief and poet,
            invented the first 7 letters,
            5 of them vowels, watching
            cranes   .   after got

The men watch and the rain does not come
        HC-108B CIVETTA LINK-BELT
In the pit below a yellow cat,
      CAT-933
      pushes the debris
and earth to load CIVETTA HC-108B
    Cat's name is PASCO and
    there is an ORegon phone number,
moves its load toward 3 piles
Let him leave the building to us

    Palamedes, son of Nauplius,
    invented   11   more
            (consonant)
    Also invented the lighthouse, and
    measures, the scales, the disc, and
    "the art of posting sentinels"
    Ruled over the Mysians,

Cretan stock, al-
though his father was Greek
Took part in the Trojan trouble on the
Greek side   .   The scholar's function is fact   .   Let him
quarry cleanly   .   All
T H O S E   I N V E N T I O N S   C R E T A N
so that a Greek   /   alpha-beta-tau
based on a Cretan, not a Phoenician
model
Three different piles:

earth   /   debris   /   & schist, the stud/stuff of the island
is moved by this
PASCO
CAT-933
ORegon 6-
it does not rain   .   smoke, the
alpha-beta-tau

raised from   5 vowels, 13 consonants to
5 vowels, 15 consonants
(Epicharmus) not
the Sicilian writer of comedies, 6 A.D., but
his ancestor   /
the Aesculapius family at Cos, a couple are
mentioned in the Iliad as physicians to
the Greeks before the equipotent walls
of Troy

No, it does not rain, smoke
rises from the engines, the
leaves   .   The men watch
before the walls of Troy

Apollo in cithaera ceteras literas adjecit
7 strings on that zither
& for each string a letter
Thence to Simonides,
native of Ceos in the service of Dionysus
which god also at home in Delphos
both gods of the solar year as were   /   Aesculapius
& Hercules
Let's
get all of this into one pot, 6-700 years B.C.

(*1* 8)

Simonides, well-known poet, intro-
duced into Athens 4 more letters   .   the
        unnecessary double-consonants *PSI*
                                        (earlier written Pi-Sigma)
        and *XI* (earlier written Kappa-Sigma)
plus (plus) two vowels : *OMEGA*, a distinction from
        the omicron Hermes conned
        from the 3 Crones, and
EPSILON, as distinct from their eta
& that's the long & the short of it .

Cranes fly in V-formation & the
Tyrrhenians, or Etruscans, were
also of Cretan stock, held
the crane in reverence   /   The men watch
                        LINK-BELT move up its load, the
                        pile to the left near 24th St., the
                        permanent erection moves
                        slow-ly, almost sensually, al-most
                                        gracefully
The scholar's function   /   fact   .   Let him quarry
cleanly   /   leave the building to us   /   Poems
nicked with a knife onto the bark of a stick (Hesiod)
        or upon tablets of clay
                    Perseus cuts off the Gorgon-head
                        (Medusa)
                    and carries it off in a bag   .   But
the head's a ritual mask and a protection, we
frighten children with it
and trespassers
when we perform the rites . It is
                        no murder,
                        she has given him power of sight
p o e t r y ,
            the gorgons no pursuers
            are escort, and the mask
                        (his protection)
Hermes / Car / Mercury / Perseus / Palamedes / Thoth / or
        whatever his original name was,
winged sandals and helmet, you bet!
the swiftness of poetic thought   /   And the bag

                                        (1 9)

THE ALPHABET'S IN THE BAG!

Almost sensually, almost
gracefully   .   The men watch
and know not what they watch
The cat pushes   .   the crane   .   the bud
lifts upward   .   above the

                     Pillars of Hercules, desti-
nation, where he is going, bringing the secret in the bag
             The tree at Gades (Cádiz)
      principal city of Tartessus, the
Aegean colony on the Guadalquivir
From there the Milesians will take it to Ireland?
The older city is on the western shore with its
            Temple of Cronus   .   island,
           the island of the goddess,
          Red Island   /   & Cronus
god of the middle finger, the fool's finger   /   It is
      his father he kills not his mother, his mother
      gives him
            the secret
              Scholar's function is
                  The men watch

Hercules' shrine set up by colonists, 1100 B.C.
400 years before the Phoenicians
coming from Tyre in painted ships
     and their oracle
             HERCULES = PALAMEDES (?)

7 & 2
9 steps to the goddess
& everyone lives to 110 years
5 years to a lustrum
             (Etruscan)
22   lustra = 110
             (alpha-beta-tau)
& the circumference of the circle when
    the diameter is   7   is
22

proportion known as π
22 (plus) over 7
a neat recurrent sequence
which does not work out because it never
ends /
7   lustra is 35 years .   Maturity,
or the age at which a man may be elected
President of the United States / a convention
or a Roman might be elected Consul / a convention

$$\frac{22}{7}$$

These numbers no longer a secret /   But in Crete
                                      or Spain . . .

Spanish, the mother's family name
still is set down last, and
still in Crete descent is matrilineal
The Greeks have accomplished nothing
        but death   beauty
              (Troy)
The men watch the cat push
keeping the piles discrete
earth /   debris / & schist
the stuff of the island, the crane, the bud
lifts upward .   above the

                    And at Cádiz, Caius Julius Hyginus,
                    a Spaniard and Ovid's friend,
                    curator of the Palantine Library,
                    exiled from the court of Augustus

sitting under a tree in Cádiz
over the problem, over a millennium later,
traces Greek letters in the spelt of wine at his table
watches the cranes fly over toward Africa
wedge in the sunset /   set down the score :

                    Mercury (or the Fates) 7
                    Palamedes   11
                    Epicharmus   2
                    Simonides   4
Say that he used Etruscan sources,
        does that explain it?

                                        (21)

Let them quarry cleanly
        Let them leave
Cranes winging over toward Africa
            a wedge .
Hyginus traces π on the wooden table in wine spelt

        The cat pushes, the crane, the bud
        lifts upward   /   above the
        rain comes finally
The watchers leave the construction site,
the men leave their machines
        At 323 Third Avenue
        an old drunk (Hyginus)
sits in a doorway and downs a whole
pint of Sacramento Tomato Juice

                                The watchers are the gods

                                The leaves burgeon

THOMAS BLACKBURN

An Aftermath

They hadn't noticed her coming, too busy with loud
Out-goings, that savage night, his wife and he;
Two's company, you know, but three's a crowd,
And the upthrust and draught of fantasy
Leave little room a child can hope to fill.
Evil each saw and nothing else could see,
The two of them were dead if looks could kill;
And then they turned and saw her balanced there
Upon the spinning rim of their nightmare.

I'd like to think it shook them to a pause,
Their daughter, her shut face, but that's not true;
Nothing mattered to them but an antique ghost,
And the open rent in their sides it cackled through.
One can imagine what sly words they said
To shrug the violence off and half explain
A foundered world, then pack her off to bed;
Speed was what counted, they'd to fight again
Within a ring they tried to think their own—
Making the darkness where she lay alone.

Such smilings, though, on the morning after that night!
Red-handed both of them, they groped for chat—
It's easy to make darkness but not light—
He pointed out the business of some cat,
There on the lawn, the feathers of a bird,
But knew she knew the game that they'd been at:
Those burnt out eyes of her had never stirred
From what between them in the night occurred.

"A door," he murmured, "a door bruised mother's eye?"
She stared of course clean through that question mark,
Puzzled he'd offered her a half-baked lie.
Like cats, he thought, a child sees through the dark,
And, with no adult technique of escape,
Runs the bad gauntlet of its parents' dream:
What is a fitting panacea for rape?
Strawberries I think they offered and whipped cream;
Within that garden where the shapes of night
Still prowled about them in the June sunlight.

As bedtime came, he sensed her terror grow;
Would it rise again, the petroleum sea, and pluck
Their features away in its savage undertow;
Must she ride their beaten minds down gulfs of shock?
She undergoes, he thought, what we've undergone—
Remembering, himself a child, how the house would rock—
Will this circle of revenants never, never be done,
Must ever the haunted ones to haunt come back?
He turned and saw his daughter was asleep,
His wife beside her in the faint blue air;
It seems as well as furies of the deep,
Moments of clarity we also share.

(23)

Poem Against the Rich

Each day I live, each day the sea of light
Rises, I seem to see
The tear inside the stone
As if my eyes were gazing beneath the earth.
The rich man in his red hat
Cannot hear
The weeping in the pueblos of the lily,
Or the dark tears in the shacks of the corn.
Each day the sea of light rises
I hear the sad rustle of the darkened armies,
Where each man weeps, and the plaintive
Orisons of the stones.
The stones bow as the saddened armies pass.

Snowfall in the Afternoon

I

The grass is half-covered with snow.
It was the sort of snowfall that starts in late afternoon,
And now the little houses of the grass are growing dark.

II

If I reached my hands down, near the earth,
I could take handfuls of darkness!
A darkness was always there, which we never noticed.

III

As the snow grows heavier, the cornstalks fade farther away,
And the barn moves nearer to the house.
The barn moves all alone in the growing storm.

The barn is full of corn, and moving toward us now,
Like a hulk blown toward us in a storm at sea;
All the sailors on deck have been blind for many years.

EDWIN BROCK

To My Mother

"I went to dances when I carried you . . .
"your father charlestoned like a movie star . . .
"six months gone I was before they knew . . .
"my skirts were short and I wore shingled hair . . ."

Thus my mother leads me curling back
in confidence in quiet afternoons
along a past that history has cracked
and cul-de-sac-ed in four unfurnished rooms

and twenty years have heard the words again,
in lieu of any other liturgy,
in plainsong that is neither song nor plain
but evidence of that reality
in which, for six short months, my mother lives
her prayer: that God repents what she forgives.

The Curtain Poem

A home should have a wife, a cat
and blinds upon the windows that
when pulled aside are suddenly drawn back
again. A wife should have a cat to kick

a home to love and, if I have not made
my meaning plain, a curtain to be drawn
aside and suddenly pulled back again.

A man should have a wife to love
a home to kick and cats upon the curtains which
he may from time to time refrain
from seizing to and back again.

But if a home should have a man
who waits upon a window-sill
endeavoring to find a plan
for all that moves outside the pane

be sure the home will have a wife
perhaps the wife will have a cat
but if by now my meaning is not plain
the wife in all sincerity should

turn her back upon the scream
and, singing, seize the cloth across again.

Catastrophe

I destroyed the first cat we had:
crammed her into a basket one spring-wet
day and walked angrily to the vet. "Do away
with her," I said. "For a year we've tried
to train her, and the flat is full of fishbones
and catshit." The second cat, a small grey
one that I loved, pined for the first one
and died a month later. After that
there were a succession of cats, dying
from cat-flu, dysentery, pregnancy
and motor cars. I suppose we were fond of them.

If the first cat had lived, the second one
would not have died; nor would the others
have followed. There are times
when I feel a kind of Eichmann of cats,

and pray that it will not be the same
with wives. Whether she destroyed me
or I her is irrelevant. She must not be
the first to die of treachery, adultery,
pregnancy or suicide. One could easily
acquire a taste for this kind of living.
I watch the way I treat my children—carefully.

HAYDEN CARRUTH

On a Certain Engagement South of Seoul

A long time, many years, we've had these wars.
When they were opened, one can scarcely say.
We were high school students, no more than sophomores,

When Italy broke her peace on a dark day,
And that was not the beginning. The following years
Grew crowded with destruction and dismay.

When I was nineteen, once the surprising tears
Stood in my eyes and stung me, for I saw
A soldier in a newsreel clutch his ears

To hold his face together. Those that paw
The public's bones to eat the public's heart
Said far too much, of course. The sight, so raw

And unbelievable, of people blown apart
Was enough to numb us without that bark and whine.
We grew disconsolate. Each had his chart

To mark on the kitchen wall the battle-line,
But many were out of date. The radio
Droned through the years, a faithful anodyne.

Yet the news of this slight encounter somewhere below
Seoul stirs my remembrance: we were a few,
Sprawled on the stiff grass of a small plateau,

Afraid. No one was dead. But we were new—
We did not know that probably none would die.
Slowly, then, all vision went askew.

My clothing was outlandish; earth and sky
Were metallic and horrible. We were unreal,
Strange bodies and alien minds; we could not cry

For even our eyes seemed to be made of steel;
Nor could we look at one another, for each
Was a sign of fear, and we could not conceal

Our hatred for our friends. There was no speech.
We sat alone, all of us, trying to wake
Some memory of the selves beyond our reach.

That place was conquered. The nations undertake
Another campaign now, in another land,
A stranger land perhaps. And we forsake

The miseries there that we can't understand
Just as we always have. And yet my glimpse
Of a scene on the distant field can make my hand

Tremble again. How quiet we are. One limps.
One cannot walk at all. Or one is all right.
But one owns this experience that crimps

Forgetfulness, especially at night.
Is this a bond? Does this make us brothers?
Or does it bring our hatred back? I might

Have known, but now I do not know. Others
May know. I know when I walk out-of-doors
I have a sorrow not wholly mine, but another's.

Keraunograph

Night-piercing, whitely illuminant,
The lightning flees but leaves
A pale secret of trees in leaping
Attitudes.

Mind sears in the storm's disclosure:
This is no image of a peopled
Forest.

Earth in its power exultant,
Clamant in praises, unweariable,
Sufficient.

The scar is deep. We, the brief
Strangers, wondering at our loneliness,
Catch sight of the local mysteries,
The rites uninterrupted by our arrival
Or departure.

CHARLES CAUSLEY

On Seeing a Poet of the First World War on the Station at Abbeville

Poet, cast your careful eye
Where the beached songs of summer lie,
    White fell the wave that splintered
    The wreck where once you wintered,
White as the snows that lair
Your freezing hair.

Captain, here you took your wine,
The trees at ease in the orchard-line,
    Bonny the errand-boy bird
    Whistles the songs you once heard,
While you traverse the wire,
Autumn will hold her fire.

Through the tall wood the thunder ran
As when the gibbering guns began,
    Swift as a murderer by the stack
    Crawled the canal with fingers black,
Black with your brilliant blood
You lit the mud.

Two grey moths stare from your eyes,
Sharp is your sad face with surprise.
    In the stirring pool I fail
    To see the drowned of Passchendaele,
Where all day drives for me
The spoiling sea.

JOHN   CIARDI

The Gift

In 1945, when the keepers cried *kaput*,
Josef Stein, poet, came out of Dachau
like half a resurrection, his other
eighty pounds still in their invisible grave.

Slowly then the mouth opened and first
a broth, and then a medication, and then
a diet, and all in time and the knitting mercies,
the showing bones were buried back in flesh,

and the miracle was finished. Josef Stein,
man and poet, rose, walked, and could even
beget, and did, and died later of other causes
only partly traceable to his first death.

He noted—with some surprise at first—
that strangers could not tell he had died once.
He returned to his post in the library, drank his beer,
published three poems in a French magazine,

and was very kind to the son who at last was his.
In the spent of one night he wrote three propositions:
That Hell is the denial of the ordinary. That nothing lasts.
That clean white paper waiting under a pen

is the gift beyond history and hurt and heaven.

AUSTIN CLARKE

Ancient Lights

When all of us wore smaller shoes
And knew the next world better than
The knots we broke, I used to hurry
On missions of my own to Capel
Street, Bolton Street and Granby Row
To see what man has made. But darkness
Was roomed with fears. Sleep, stripped by woes
I had been taught, beat door, leaped landing,
Lied down the bannisters of naught.

Being sent to penance, come Saturday,
I shuffled slower than my sins should.
My fears were candle-spiked at side-shrines,
Rays lengthened them in stained-glass. Confided
To night again, my grief bowed down,

Heard hand on shutter-knob. Did I
Take pleasure, when alone—how much—
In a bad thought, immodest look
Or worse, unnecessary touch?

Closeted in the confessional,
I put on flesh, so many years
Were added to my own, attempted
In vain to keep Dominican
As much i' the dark as I was, mixing
Whispered replies with his low words;
Then shuddered past the crucifix,
The feet so hammered, daubed-on blood-drip,
Black with lip-scrimmage of the damned.

Once as I crept from the church-steps,
Beside myself, the air opened
On purpose. Nature read in a flutter
An evening lesson above my head.
Atwirl beyond the leadings, corbels,
A cage-bird came among sparrows
(The moral inescapable)
Plucked, roof-mired, all in mad bits. O
The pizzicato of its wires!

Goodness of air can be proverbial:
That day, by the kerb at Rutland Square,
A bronze bird fabled out of trees,
Mailing the spearheads of the railings,
Sparrow at nails, I hailed the skies
To save the tiny dropper, found
Appetite gone. A child of clay
Has blustered it away. Pity
Could raise some littleness from dust.

What Sunday clothes can change us now
Or humble orders in black and white?
Stinking with centuries the act
Of thought. So think man, as Augustine
Did, dread the ink-bespattered ex-monk,
And keep your name. No, let me abandon

Night's jakes. Self-persecuted of late
Among the hatreds of rent Europe,
Poetry burns at a different stake.

Still, still I remember aweful downpour
Cabbing Mountjoy Street, spun loneliness
Veiling almost the Protestant church,
Two backyards from my very home.
I dared to shelter at locked door.
There, walled by heresy, my fears
Were solved. I had absolved myself:
Feast-day effulgence, as though I gained
For life a plenary indulgence.

The sun came out, new smoke flew up,
The gutters of the Black Church rang
With services. Waste water mocked
The ballcocks: down-pipes sparrowing,
And all around the spires of Dublin
Such swallowing in the air, such cowling
To keep high offices pure: I heard,
From shore to shore, the iron gratings
Take half our heavens with a roar.

Respectable People

Thought rattles along the empty railings
Of street and square they lived in, years
Ago. I dream of them at night,
Strangers to this artificial light,
Respectable people who gave me sweets,
Talked above my head or unfobbed
The time. I know them by each faded
Smile and their old-fashioned clothes.
But how can I make room for them
In a mind too horrible with life?
This is the last straw in the grave,
Propping the tear in which grief burns
Away. Shame of eternity

Has stripped them of their quiet habits,
Unshovelled them out of the past.
Memory finds beyond that last
Improvidence, their mad remains.

The Envy of Poor Lovers

Pity poor lovers who may not do what they please
With their kisses under a hedge, before a raindrop
Unhouses it; and astir from wretched centuries,
Bramble and briar remind them of the saints.

Her envy is the curtain seen at night-time,
Happy position that could change her name.
His envy—clasp of the unmarried whose thoughts can be alike,
Whose nature flows without the blame or shame.

Lying in the grass as if it were a sin
To move, they hold each other's breath, tremble,
Ready to share that ancient dread—kisses begin
Again—of Ireland keeping company with them.

Think, children, of institutions mured above
Your ignorance, where every look is veiled,
State-paid to snatch away the folly of poor lovers
For whom, it seems, the sacraments have failed.

Intercessors

Our nuns come out to shop in the afternoon,
For holy fashion has decreed hold-alls.
Torchbearers sidle the clergy to their stalls
To share in the dark, huge hug, comic cartoon,
Forget awhile the morning fast in croon
Of saxophone. Free from the pledge of walls,
Passing the beggar-women who still wear shawls,
Capuchin pads in mediaeval shoon.
These are our intercessors. Strange that hotel
Lounge, cinema, shop-window can unbell

Them! Flattered by their numbers and display,
We break their vows with a smile. No rebel guessed
Prayer and retreat would sanctify unrest,
When Britain took the garrisons away.

ROBERT CONQUEST

On the Danube

(I)

The convicts working on the frontier forts
Have been marched back. The palpable cool air
Of evening lies round me now. A single peasant
Passes unsteadily, reeking of plum brandy,
And then I am alone.

　　　　　　　The day pauses. The great river
Slides softly by towards the delta and the sea;
And now the sun strikes from an unaccustomed angle
And the light changes:

　　　　　　　always at this hour
And in such scenery I wait for revelation,
Under a sky as pale as mother-of-pearl.
It is not that this pure moment can admit
A supernatural vision to the unclear heart,
But it hides the worn planet with its freshness;
The light is no more absolute, but only
Closer to some untried colour of the air,
And there flickers round the horizons of my heart
The brilliance that precedes a greater brilliance.

(II)

The winds of Europe and of tragedy
Are filling the sails of poetry here and everywhere.

(35)

And I wonder now in what tall uncaused singer
This rich and bitter land warms out.

                      Last night
In a little inn beside the landing-stage
A young man was writing verses at a table
And eating sturgeon stuffed with aubergines.
And perhaps he was the poet for whom the Balkans wait,
Though this is hardly likely.

                     The day before
I saw him reading Marx on a bench beside the river,
The witty laboured blue-prints for perfected anarchy,
Now legal in this country. (The social sky
Holds only now his dialectic for its sun,
But I find a shade by the poetic tree
Under a moon of love.)

                    Night has fallen,
A young heron rises awkwardly into the air
Under the vague starlight, heading west.
The river ripples as some big fish dives.
And I walk back to the inn.

                      The moon is rising.

(III)

I stumble over a machine-gun tripod
Half-buried in the sand. It is now almost eight months
Since the S.S. Regiment "Turkestan"
Was brought to battle here, surrounded and destroyed,
And a cold complexity of violence still
Lies heavy on this broken continent,
Which these bronze waters and this natural night
Can never answer.

                Yet here I am alone and far
From the brilliance of the fighting ideologies,
And I think of a girl in a small provincial town
Looking through a spring rain and imagining love.

The Saints

Heaven won't have to do with its multitudes.
There isn't room enough.
A thought we've all had perhaps,
now taken beyond that consideration.

Last night I saw several people
in a dream, in shapes
of all of this: faces and hands,
and things to say, too.

I love you, one said.
And I love you too. Let's
get out of this.
One said: I have to take a piss.

The door to the pantry was dark,
where the two crouched,
his hand on her back, her hand
on his back. I looked

at an evil, in the face.
I saw its place, in the universe,
and laughed back
until my mind cracked.

Sing Song

I sing the song of the sleeping wife,
who married to sleep,
who would not sleep simply to get married;

who can be up at dawn, yet
never cannot go to sleep if there is
good reason not to go to sleep;

who sleeps to sleep,
who has no other purpose in mind,
who wouldn't even hear you if you asked her.

Kore

As I was walking
   I came upon
chance walking
   the same road upon.

As I sat down
   by chance to move
later
   if and as I might,

light the wood was,
   light and green,
and what I saw
   before I had not seen.

It was a lady
   accompanied
by goat men
   leading her.

Her hair held earth.
   Her eyes were dark.
A double flute
   made her move.

"O love,
   where are you
leading
   me now?"

J. V. CUNNINGHAM

Interview with Doctor Drink

I have a fifth of therapy
In the house, and transference there.
Doctor, there's not much wrong with me,
Only a sick rattlesnake somewhere

In the house, if it be there at all,
But the lithe mouth is coiled. The shapes
Of door and window move. I call.
What is it that pulls down the drapes,

Disheveled and exposed? Your rye
Twists in my throat: intimacy
Is like hard liquor. Who but I
Coil there and squat, and pay your fee?

DONALD DAVIE

The Wind at Penistone

The wind meets me at Penistone.
                     A hill
Curves empty through the township, on a slope
Not cruel, and yet steep enough to be,
Were it protracted, cruel.
                In the street,
A plain-ness rather meagre than severe,
Affords, though quite unclassical, a vista
So bald as to be monumental.

(39)

Here

A lean young housewife meets me with the glance
I like to think that I can recognize
As dour, not cross.
     And all the while the wind,
A royal catspaw, toying easily,
Flicks out of shadows from a tufted wrist,
Its mane, perhaps, this lemon-coloured sun.

The wind reserves, the hill reserves, the style
Of building houses on the hill reserves
A latent edge;
     which we can do without
In Pennine gradients and the Pennine wind,
And never miss or, missing it, applaud
The absence of the aquiline;
       which in her
Whose style of living in the wind reserves
An edge to meet the wind's edge, we may miss
But without prejudice.
     And yet in art
Where all is patent, and a latency
Is manifest or nothing, even I,
Liking to think I feel these sympathies,
Can hardly praise this clenched and muffled style.

For architecture asks a cleaner edge,
Is open-handed.
     And close-fisted people
Are mostly vulgar; only in the best,
Who draw, inflexible, upon reserves,
Is there a stern game that they play with life,
In which the rule is not to show one's hand
Until compelled.
     And then the lion's paw!
Art that is dour and leonine in the Alps
Grows kittenish, makes curios and clocks,
Giant at play.
     Here, nothing. So the wind
Meets me at Penistone, and, coming home,
The poet falls to special pleading, chilled
To find in Art no fellow but the wind.

(4 0)

New York in August

After Pasternak

There came, for lack of sleep,
A crosspatch, drained-out look
On the old trees that keep
Scents of Schiedam and the Hook

In Flushing, as we picked out, past
Each memorised landmark,
Our route to a somnolent breakfast.
Later, to Central Park,

UNO, and the Empire State.
A haven from the heat
Was the Planetarium. We got back late,
Buffeted, dragging our feet.

Clammy, electric, torrid,
The nights bring no relief
At the latitude of Madrid.
Never the stir of a leaf

Any night, as we went
Back, the children asleep,
To our bed in a loaned apartment,
Although I thought a deep

And savage cry from the park
Came once, as we flashed together
And the fan whirled in the dark,
For thunder, a break in the weather.

For Doreen

We have a lawn of moss.
The next house is called The Beeches.
Its towering squirrel-haunted
Trellis of trees, across

(41)

Our matt and trefoil, reaches
Shade where our guests have sauntered.

Cars snap by in the road.
In a famous photographed village
The High Street is our address.
Our guests write from abroad
Delighted to envisage
Rose-arbour and wilderness.

They get them, and the lilacs.
Some frenzy in us discards
Lilacs and all. It will harden,
However England stacks
Her dear discoloured cards
Against us, us to her garden.

Anglophobia rises
In Brooklyn to hysteria
At some British verses.
British, one sympathizes.
Diesel-fumes cling to wistaria.
One conceives of worse reverses.

The sough of the power brake
Makes every man an island,
But we are the island race.
We must be mad to take
Offence at our poisoned land
And the gardens that pock her face.

Ballad of Mistress Death

"OH, I've had ten men before you,"
Said my redhead Sally,
"Yes, and a hundred men before you,"
Said my new-found darling.
The sea's blue maw glittered
Like a fat, barbaric queen's
And her thighs were white and gold
Like wisp-rain in sunshine.

In the long hall with statues
We sat and were not lonely,
Her name all forgotten,
My darkhead, my darling
Said in a gentle voice:
"And you never will be jealous
Though many's the man's head
Has lain upon my pillow,
For you've found out my secret
And many's the man more will."

"Yes, I've found out your secret,"
Said I to my darling,
Walking the dark streets
Through leaf-shaken lamplight.
"I never will be jealous
Nor you numb or nag at me
I'll name you the world's most beauty
Yellowheaded Helen
And no lie be telling;
No woman will disprove it."

She held me like nightfall
Her breath came like knives
While the housing plains sank lower
With their cinder-grates of cities—
Oh, there will need no porters
When all those doors open!

The Being

I

It is there, above him, beyond, behind,

Distant, and near where he lies in his sleep
Bound down as for warranted torture.
Through his eyelids he sees it

Drop off its wings or its clothes.
He groans, and breaks almost from

Or into another sleep.
Something fills the bed he has been
Able only to half-fill.

He turns and buries his head.

II

Moving down his back,
Back up his back,
Is an infinite, unworldly frankness,
Showing him what an entire

Possession nakedness is.
Something over him

Is praying.
                 It reaches down under
His eyelids and gently lifts them.
He expects to look straight into eyes
And to see thereby through the roof.

III

Darkness. The window-pane stirs.
His lids close again, and the room

(44)

Begins to breathe on him
As through the eyeholes of a mask.

The praying of prayer
Is not in the words but the breath.
It sees him and touches him
All over, from everywhere.
It lifts him from the mattress
To be able to flow around him

In the heat from a coal-bed burning
Far under the earth.
He enters—enters with . . .
What? His tongue? A word?

His own breath? Some part of his body?
All.
                                    None.

He lies laughing silently
In the dark of utter delight.

IV

It glides, glides
Lightly over him, over his chest and legs.
All breath is called suddenly back

Out of laughter and weeping at once.
His face liquefies and freezes

Like a mask. He goes rigid
And breaks into sweat from his heart
All over his body
In something's hands.

V

He sleeps, and the window-pane
Ceases to flutter.
Frost crawls down off it
And backs into only
The two bottom corners of glass.

(45)

VI

He stirs, with the sun held at him
Out of late-winter dawn, and blazing
Levelly into his face.
He blazes back with his eyes closed,
Given, also, renewed

Fertility, to raise
Dead plants and sleep-walking beasts
Out of their thawing holes,

And children up,
From mortal women or angels,
As true to themselves as he

Is only in visited darkness
For one night out of the year,

And as he is now, seeing straight
Through the roof, wide, wider,

Wide awake.

ALAN DUGAN

Memorial Service for the Invasion Beach
Where the Vacation in the Flesh is Over

I see that there it is on the beach. It is
ahead of me and I walk toward it: its
following vultures and contemptible dogs
are with it, and I walk toward it. If,
in the approach to it, I turn my back
to it, then I walk backwards: I
approach it as a limit. Even if I fall
to hands and knees, I crawl to it.
Backwards or forwards I approach it.

There is the land on one hand, rising, and
the ocean on the other, falling away;
what the sky does, I can not look to see,
but it's around, as ever, all around.
The courteous vultures move away in groups
like functionaries. The dogs circle and stare
like working police. One wants a heel
and gets it. I approach it, concentrating so
on not approaching it, going so far away
that when I get there I am sideways like
the crab, too limited by carapace to say:
"Oh here I am arrived, all; yours today."
No: kneeling and facing away, I will
fall over backwards in intensity of life
and lie convulsed, downed struggling,
sideways even, and should a vulture ask
an eye as its aperitif, I grant it,
glad for the moment wrestling by a horse
whose belly has been hollowed from the rear,
who's eyeless. The wild dog trapped in its ribs
grins as it eats its way to freedom. Not
conquered outwardly, and after rising once,
I fall away inside, and see the sky around
rush out away into the vulture's craw
and barely can not hear them calling, "Here's one."

How We Heard the Name

The river brought down
dead horses, dead men
and military debris,
indicative of war
or official acts upstream,
but it went by, it all
goes by, that is the thing
about the river. Then
a soldier on a log
went by. He seemed drunk

and we asked him why
had he and this junk
come down to us so
from the past upstream.
"Friends," he said, "the great
Battle of Granicus
has just been won
by all of the Greeks except
the Lacedaemonians and
myself: this is a joke
between me and a man
named Alexander, whom
all of you ba-bas
will hear of as a god."

ROBERT DUNCAN

Often I Am Permitted to Return to a Meadow

as if it were a scene made-up by the mind,
that is not mine, but is a made place,

that is mine, it is so near to the heart,
an eternal pasture folded in all thought
so that there is a hall therein

that is made place, created by light
wherefrom the shadows that are forms fall.

Wherefrom fall all architectures I am
I say are likenesses of the First Beloved
whose flowers are flames lit to the Lady.

(4 8)

She is Queen Under The Hill
whose hosts are a disturbance of words within words
that is a field folded.

It is only a dream of the grass blowing
east against the source of the sun
in an hour before the sun's going down

whose secret we see in a children's game
of ring a round of roses told.

Often I am permitted to return to a meadow
as if it were a given property of the mind
that certain bounds hold against chaos,

that is a place of first permission,
everlasting omen of what is.

FROM *A Poem Beginning with a Line by Pindar*

I

The light foot hears you and the brightness begins
god-step at the margins of thought,
   quick adulterous tread at the heart.
Who is it that goes there?
   Where I see your quick face
notes of an old music pace the air,
torso-reverberations of a Grecian lyre.

In Goya's canvas Cupid and Psyche
have a hurt voluptuous grace
bruised by redemption. The copper light
falling upon the brown boy's slight body
is carnal fate that sends the soul wailing
up from blind innocence, ensnared
   by dimness
into the deprivations of desiring sight.

But the eyes in Goya's painting are soft,
diffuse with rapture absorb the flame.

(*49*)

Their bodies yield out of strength.
    Waves of visual pleasure
wrap them in a sorrow previous to their impatience.

A bronze of yearning, a rose that burns
    the tips of their bodies, lips,
ends of fingers, nipples. He is not wingd.
His thighs are flesh, are clouds
    lit by the sun in its going down,
hot luminescence at the loins of the visible.

    But they are not in a landscape.
    They exist in an obscurity.

The wind spreading the sail serves them.
The two jealous sisters eager for her ruin
    serve them.
That she is ignorant, ignorant of what Love will be,
    serves them.
The dark serves them.
The oil scalding his shoulder serves them,
serves their story. Fate, spinning,
    knots the threads for Love.

Jealousy, ignorance, the hurt . . . serve them.

II

This is magic. It is passionate dispersion.
What if they grow old? The gods
    would not allow it.
    Psyche is preserved.

In time we see a tragedy, a loss of beauty
    the glittering youth
of the god retains—but from this threshold
    it is age
that is beautiful. It is toward the old poets
    we go, to their faltering,
their unaltering wrongness that has style,
    their variable truth,
    the old faces,
words shed like tears from
a plenitude of powers time stores.

A stroke. These little strokes. A chill.
   The old man, feeble, does not recoil.
Recall. A phase so minute,
   only a part of the word in- jerrd.

   The Thundermakers descend,

damerging a nuv. A nerb.
   The present dented of the U
nighted stayd. States. The heavy clod?
   Cloud. Invades the brain. What
   if lilacs last in *this* dooryard bloomd?

Hoover, Roosevelt, Truman, Eisenhower—
where among these did the power reside
that moves the heart? What flower of the nation
bride-sweet broke to the whole rapture?
Hoover, Coolidge, Harding, Wilson
hear the factories of human misery turning out commodities.
For whom are the holy matins of the heart ringing?
Noble men in the quiet of morning hear
Indians singing the continent's violent requiem.
Harding, Wilson, Taft, Roosevelt,
idiots fumbling at the bride's door,
hear the cries of men in meaningless debt and war.
Where among these did the spirit reside
that restores the land to productive order?
McKinley, Cleveland, Harrison, Arthur,
Garfield, Hayes, Grant, Johnson,
swell in the roots of the heart's rancor.
How sad "amid lanes and through old woods"
   echoes Whitman's love for Lincoln!

There is no continuity then. Only a few
   posts of the good remain. I too
that am a nation sustain the damage
   where smokes of continual ravage
obscure the flame.
                     It is across great scars of wrong
   I reach toward the song of kindred men
   and strike again the naked string
old Whitman sang from. Glorious mistake!
   that cried:

"The theme is creative and has vista."
"He is the president of regulation."

I see always the under side turning,
fumes that injure the tender landscape.
    From which up break
lilac blossoms of courage in daily act
    striving to meet a natural measure.

Ingmar Bergman's Seventh Seal

This is the way it is. We see
three ages in one: the child Jesus
innocent of Jerusalem and Rome
—magically at home in joy—
that's the year from which
our inner persistence has its force.

The second, Bergman shows us,
carries forward image after image
of anguish, of the Christ crossd
and sends up from open sores of the plague
(shown as wounds upon His corpse)
from lacerations in the course of love
(the crown of whose kingdom tears the flesh)

. . . There is so much suffering!
What possibly protects us
from the emptiness, the forsaken cry,
the utter dependence, the vertigo?
Why do so many come to love's edge
only to be stranded there?

The second face of Christ, his
evil, his Other, emaciated, pain and sin.
Christ, what a contagion!
What a stink it spreads round

our age! It's our age!
and the rage of the storm is abroad.
The malignant stupidity of statesmen rules.
The old riders thru the forests race
    shouting: the wind! the wind!
Now the black horror cometh again.

And I'll throw myself down
As the clown does in Bergman's *Seventh Seal*
to cower as if asleep with his wife and child,
hid in the caravan under the storm.
Let the Angel of Wrath pass over.
Let the end come.
War, stupidity and fear are powerful.
We are only children. To bed! to bed!
    To play safe!

To throw ourselves down
helplessly, into happiness,
    into an age of our own, into
    our own days.
There where the Pestilence roars,
where the empty riders of the horror go.

Strains of Sight

1

He brought a light so she could see
Adam move nakedly in the lighted room.
It was a window in the tree.
It was a shelter where there was none.

She saw his naked back and thigh
and heard the notes of a melody
where Adam out of his nature came
into four walls, roof and floor.

He turnd on the light and turnd back,
moving with grace to catch her eye.
She saw his naked loneliness.

(53)

Now I shall never rest, she sighd,
until he strips his heart for me.
The body flashes such thoughts of death
so that time leaps up, and a man's hand

seen naked catches upon my breath
the risk we took in Paradise.
The serpent thought before the tomb
laid naked, naked, naked before the eyes,

reflects upon itself in a bare room.

2

In the questioning phrase the voice
—he raises his eyes from the page—
follows towards some last
curve of the air, suspended above

its sign, that point, that.
And asks, Who am I then?
Where am I going? There is no time
like now that is not like now.

Who?   turns upon some body where
the hand striving to tune
curves of the first lute whose strings are nerves
sees in the touch the phrase will

rise   .   break
as the voice does? above some moving obscurity

ripples out in the disturbd pool,
shadows and showings where we would read
—raising his eyes from the body's lure—

what the question is,
where the heart reflects.

RICHARD EBERHART

The Fury of Aerial Bombardment

You would think the fury of aerial bombardment
Would rouse God to relent; the infinite spaces
Are still silent. He looks on shock-pried faces.
History, even, does not know that is meant.

You would feel that after so many centuries
God would give man to repent; yet he can kill
As Cain could, but with multitudinous will,
No farther advanced than in his ancient furies.

Was man made stupid to see his own stupidity?
Is God by definition indifferent, beyond us all?
Is the eternal truth man's fighting soul
Wherein the Beast ravens in its own avidity?

Of Van Wettering I speak, and Averill,
Names on a list, whose faces I do not recall
But they are gone to early death, who late in school
Distinguished the belt feed lever from the belt holding pawl.

Vast Light

The fighting nature of the intellect,
The loving nature of the heart,
The head that hits, the blood that lets,
The lift, and the abandonment,

Concern us not fitfully, in no abatement,
Speak to us not evenly, advance
Our good in no equal certainties,
Prevail without finalities,

As when we dare not speak out for justice
Having too fine a sense of discrimination,
Or as we do not know what to do
Speculating upon the imprecision of action,

While time rolls over the richest meadows.
It is now the soul rolls over us.
It is the soul between the head and the heart
Is our air-borne master and our hair-shirt.

It is the soul that cannot be put into words
Is the word of control. Like it or not,
The soul is all that is left of time:
We see through it: we breathe it out.

I have come back to old streets at nightfall
After journeys among volcanoes and icebergs.
I have been up in sidereal glows,
I have eaten of the chill taunt of the spirit.

Whether I apply to the light of reason,
Or feed on insatiable night,
I am aware of light and vastness,
It is the vague of the soul that I know.

D. J. ENRIGHT

Apocalypse

"After the New Apocalypse, very few members were still in possession
of their instruments. Hardly a musician could call a decent suit his own.
Yet by the early summer of 1945, strains of sweet music floated on the
air again. While the town still reeked of smoke, charred buildings and
the stench of corpses, the Philharmonic Orchestra bestowed the everlasting and imperishable joy which music never fails to give."
—from *The Muses on the Banks of the Spree,*
a Berlin tourist brochure

It soothes the savage doubts.
One Bach outweighs ten Belsens. If 200,000 people
Were remaindered at Hiroshima, the sales of So-and-So's
new novel reached a higher figure in as short a time.
So, imperishable paintings reappeared:
Texts were reprinted:
Public buildings reconstructed:
Human beings reproduced.

After the Newer Apocalypse, very few members
Were still in possession of their instruments
(Very few were still in possession of their members),
And their suits were chiefly indecent.
Yet, while the town still reeked of smoke, etc.,
The Philharmonic Trio bestowed, etc.

A civilization vindicated,
A race with three legs still to stand on!
True, the violin was shortly silenced by leukaemia,
And the pianoforte crumbled softly into dust.
But the flute was left. And one is enough.
All, in a sense, goes on. All is in order.

And the ten-tongued mammoth larks,
The forty-foot crickets and the elephantine frogs
Decided that the little chap was harmless,
At least he made no noise, on the banks of whatever river it
used to be.

One day, a reed-warbler stepped on him by accident.
However, all, in a sense, goes on. Still the everlasting and
imperishable joy
Which music never fails to give is being given.

The Last Democrat

I can see him—
Drunk and roughed up, because he exercises
The right to drink, to cut up rough (a little)
And be roughed up (a lot).
I see him, and his rigorously dissipated life,
In a house full of mistresses and cats and dust
And unpaid bills (a man who liked an orderly life,
Loved peace, detested debt, was undersexed).
Conscientious patron of yellow literature,
In protest against the prim foul nursemaids
Trained in the ministries.
Because sin is democratic. Because
Virtue was being rewarded too promptly.
Determined to lead his own life, he led himself
A dance, lifted from old banned books
About Great Eccentrics.
Kept at the boil, yet his blood cools
To see his neighbours, as they look
With a plain show of their most natural feelings
At a plain straightforward malefactor.
Lecher, thief, and public nuisance.
He leers back, pulling his facial muscles,
In desperate temperance seeking a drunken curse.
Professional fallers need support. Where can he
Turn? Spawn bastard sons to carry on the fight?
(It seems he is sterile.) Better cut his throat—
Die in an old-world way to keep a principle alive.

And have the State then praise him, briefly,
As "salt of the earth" and "spice of life."
While his neighbours, in private, damn him
Freely: bad neighbour and (despite the State)
A thoroughly bad lot.

Parliament of Cats

The cats caught a Yellow-vented Bulbul.
Snatched from them, for three days it uttered
Its gentle gospel, enthroned above their heads.
Became loved and respected of all the cats.
Then succumbed to internal injuries.
The cats regretted it all profoundly,
They would never forget the evil they had done.

Later the cats caught a Daurian Starling.
And ate it. For a Daurian Starling is not
A Yellow-vented Bulbul. (Genuflection.)
Its colouring is altogether different.
It walks in a different, quite unnatural fashion.
The case is not the same at all as that of
The Yellow-vented Bulbul. (Genuflection.)

The kittens caught a Yellow-vented Bulbul.
And ate it. What difference, they ask, between
A Yellow-vented Bulbul and that known criminal
The Daurian Starling? Both move through the air
In a quite unnatural fashion. This is not
The Yellow-vented Bulbul of our parents' day,
Who was a Saint of course! (Genuflection.)

LAWRENCE FERLINGHETTI

Away above a Harborful

Away above a harborful
                              of caulkless houses
        among the charley noble chimneypots
                    of a rooftop rigged with clotheslines
                a woman pastes up sails
                              upon the wind
        hanging out her morning sheets
                              with wooden pins
                    O lovely mammal
                                    her nearly naked teats
                throw taut shadows
                              when she stretches up
        to hang at last the last of her
                              so white washed sins
                but it is wetly amorous
                              and winds itself about her
                clinging to her skin
                              So caught with arms upraised
        she tosses back her head
                              in voiceless laughter
        and in choiceless gesture then
                              shakes out gold hair

while in the reachless seascape spaces
                              between the blown white shrouds

    stand out the bright steamers

                              to kingdom come

In Goya's Greatest Scenes

In Goya's greatest scenes we seem to see
                                    the people of the world
    exactly at the moment when
          they first attained the title of
                                    'suffering humanity'
      They writhe upon the page
                          in a veritable rage
                                    of adversity
        Heaped up
                    groaning with babies and bayonets
                                        under cement skies
            in an abstract landscape of blasted trees
                bent statues bats' wings and beaks
                          slippery gibbets
              cadavers and carnivorous cocks
              and all the final hollering monsters
                  of the
                          'imagination of disaster'
              they are so bloody real
                          it is as if they really still existed

    And they do

              Only the landscape is changed

    They still are ranged along the roads
            plagued by legionaires
                          false windmills and demented roosters

    They are the same people
                          only further from home
      on freeways fifty lanes wide
                      on a concrete continent
                            spaced with bland billboards
                illustrating imbecile illusions of happiness

      The scene shows fewer tumbrils
                      but more maimed citizens
                                    in painted cars
            and they have strange license plates
            and engines
                      that devour America

                                          (61)

Orkney Interior

Doing what the moon says, he shifts his chair
Closer to the stove and stokes it up
With the very best fuel, a mixture of dried fish
And tobacco he keeps in a bucket with crabs

Too small to eat. One raises its pincer
As if to seize hold of the crescent moon
On the calendar which is almost like a zodiac
With inexplicable and pallid blanks. Meanwhile

A lobster is crawling towards the clever
Bait that is set inside the clock
On the shelf by the wireless—and inherited dried fish
Soaked in whiskey and carefully trimmed

With potato flowers from the Golden Wonders
The old man grows inside his ears.
Click! goes the clock-lid, and the unfortunate lobster
Finds itself a prisoner inside the clock,

An adapted cuckoo-clock. It shows no hours, only
Tides and moons and is fitted out
With two little saucers, one of salt and one of water
For the lobster to live on while, each quarter-tide,

It must stick its head through the tiny trapdoor
Meant for the cuckoo. It will be trained to read
The broken barometer and wave its whiskers
To Scottish Dance Music, till it grows too old.

Then the old man will have to catch himself another lobster.
Meanwhile he is happy and takes the clock
Down to the sea. He stands and oils it
In a little rock pool that reflects the moon.

Island Moment

In the still of an island evening
She goes to the big shed
Which is where she keeps the herring.
The sun—and their eyes—are red.

Past the War Memorial cycles
Her son who—O delight—
Is newly married and may count
That chest's sweet hairs now every night.

He is brown, and very tall.
If one believes the rumour
The island skulled itself to Kirkwall
Using him, Big Jim, as an oar.

Dusk is in the shed.
The long white boat is hers.
Also the yellow bamboo wand
For fishing sillocks, lithe and cuithes.

And the little herring barrel.
The light just strikes it over
Islands and miles and miles of water
That tilts to the North Pole.

AUTHOR'S NOTE: The lady of the island shop
has to go to the shore-side shed for salted
herring. It is sunset, and her son who is newly
married (and is a little set for her) is cycling
home after being at the lobsters. The hairs are
on his wife's chest: you can imagine, I hope,
that he might find them worth the counting.

(63)

The Execrators

Duck's-assed and leather-jacketed,
Dispensing shrill laughter, they tread
Lightly the pocked oval of light
In the dark street, lifting a right
Gracefully just to graze the cheek
Of the opponent, who sidles sleek
Up from under, hooking a swift,
Imaginary knife. They shift,
Then freeze into a slouch to let
The stranger dream they've never met
Or that such unity as theirs
Needs no acknowledgment. Their stares
Hide only the possibility
They will not ask the time. As he
Consults his watch, the stranger's half-
tripped, half-trips himself, on a laugh
Shaped like a boot's gleam and gone.
His tie that they admire is torn
Apart in the same breath, as are
The bills he proffers to the air.
Asked for a light, he holds the flame,
Forced, under his nose, and hears a maimed
Voice inquire if he will not please
Unzip his fly. Down on his knees,
He hugs his screaming groin. Asked where
His money is, he feels blood flare
Along his lip, a live ash break
Over his eye. "It's a mistake . . ."
He hears a voice purr, one reply,
"It always is—they never play
It dead!" Lids clenched, holding his breath,
Suddenly he brings forth a wreath
Of vomit. "What a filthy clown!"
"Look at the liar!" A pipe's brought down
Upon his teeth. His mind cuts through
The brambles of his pain to view

The broken skull it cannot fit.
What further wounds they could inflict
Would serve only to let him know
He were alive; therefore, they flow
In single file into the night.
Raked by their buttons' wolfish light,
He turns into a tree of fire
Felled, through which low laughters expire.

Ballade of the Session after Camarillo

a dead junky speaks

That was the night, Love, Bird came back and blew
In a black turban to a hall lit by candles.
Now Bird was always coming back with new
Sounds stashed inside his wig no junk could fix,
No groper handle, and over the dark
Wood a few suedes began to dust his song.
Turned on to "Billie's Bounce," we had our kicks—
Staring hard at the gold bell of a horn.
The scene was straight; a red flash left its mark
There in the light. I laughed and you were gone.

Outside: a holy night of snow. A Jew
Called Charlie Parker jammed bent on straw sandals,
In a three-cornered hat, ram's-horning the blue
Megillah of pride in his despair, the tricks
Only you and I could hear. Your dark
Obviousness to cut me, Love, signed long
Windows of my fear. Of all the chicks
You were the only one could put me down
Like Bird's line had a swinging wall to rock
There in the light. I laughed and you were gone.

My doorway shook. I gigged with a midnight crew
East, far west. The Law behind shiny handles
Crouched, like Art straightening up to rap a clue
To all our silences. A Bronx of bricks

(6 5)

Whirled from a thump of slush to maze the stark
Monster of music! Love, I did no wrong:
A line of lights reeled out between the wrecks
To blink whose Theseus I was. Till dawn
I grooved cool ever back from the world's mark
There in the light. I laughed and you were gone.

Sweet chick, I cannot blow you any song
Can make your session swing. Go have your kicks.
Buy you a black turban, if you must mourn;
Mourn all our sounds that never split from dark
There in the light. I laughed and you were gone.

JACK   GILBERT

Don Giovanni on His Way to Hell (II)

FOR SUE

How could they think women a recreation?
Or the repetition of bodies of steady interest?
Only the ignorant or busy could. That elm
Of flesh must prove a luxury of primes;
Be perilous and dear with rain of an alternate earth.
Which is not to damn the forested China of touching.
I am neither priestly nor tired, and the great knowledge
Of breasts with their loud nipples congregates in me.
The sudden nakedness, the small ribs, the mouth.
Splendid. Splendid. Splendid. Like Rome. Like loins.
A glamour sufficient to our long marvelous dying.
I say sufficient and speak with earned privilege,
For my life has been eaten in that foliate city.
To ambergris. But not for recreation.
I would not have lost so much for recreation.

(66)

Nor for love as the sweet pretend: the children's game
Of deliberate ignorance of each to allow the dreaming.
Not for the impersonal belly nor the heart's drunkenness
Have I come this far, stubborn, disastrous way.
But for relish of those archipelagoes of person.
To hold her in hand, closed as any sparrow,
And call and call forever till she turn from bird
To blowing woods. From wood to jungle. Persimmon.
To light. From light to Princess. From Princess to woman
In all her fresh particularity of difference.
Then O, through the underwater time of night,
Indecent and still, to speak to her without habit.
This I have done with my life, and am content.
I wish I could tell you how it is in that dark
Standing in the huge singing and the alien world.

ALLEN GINSBERG

America

America I've given you all and now I'm nothing.
America two dollars and twentyseven cents January 17, 1956.
I can't stand on my own mind.
America when will we end the human war?
Go fuck yourself with your atom bomb.
I don't feel good don't bother me.
I won't write my poem till I'm in my right mind.
America when will you be angelic?
When will you take off your clothes?
When will you look at yourself through the grave?
When will you be worthy of your million Trotskyites?
America why are your libraries full of tears?
America when will you send your eggs to India?
I'm sick of your insane demands.

When can I go into the supermarket and buy what I need with
my good looks?
America after all it is you and I who are perfect not the next
world.
Your machinery is too much for me.
You made me want to be a saint.
There must be some other way to settle this argument.
Burroughs is in Tangiers I don't think he'll come back it's
sinister.
Are you being sinister or is this some form of practical joke?
I'm trying to come to the point.
I refuse to give up my obsession.
America stop pushing I know what I'm doing.
America the plum blossoms are falling.
I haven't read the newspapers for months, everyday somebody
goes on trial for murder.
America I feel sentimental about the Wobblies.
America I used to be a communist when I was a kid I'm not
sorry.
I smoke marijuana every chance I get.
I sit in my house for days on end and stare at the roses in the
closet.
When I go to Chinatown I get drunk and never get laid.
My mind is made up there's going to be trouble.
You should have seen me reading Marx.
My psychoanalyst thinks I'm perfectly right.
I won't say the Lord's Prayer.
I have mystical visions and cosmic vibrations.
America I still haven't told you what you did to Uncle Max
after he came over from Russia.

I'm addressing you.
Are you going to let your emotional life be run by Time
Magazine?
I'm obsessed by Time Magazine.
I read it every week.
Its cover stares at me every time I slink past the corner candy-
store.
I read it in the basement of the Berkeley Public Library.
It's always telling me about responsibility. Businessmen are
serious. Movie producers are serious. Everybody's seri-
ous but me.

(68)

It occurs to me that I am America.
I am talking to myself again.

Asia is rising against me.
I haven't got a chinaman's chance.
I'd better consider my national resources.
My national resources consist of two joints of marijuana mil-
           lions of genitals an unpublishable private literature
           that goes 1400 miles an hour and twentyfive-thousand
           mental institutions.
I say nothing about my prisons nor the millions of under-
           privileged who live in my flowerpots under the light
           of five hundred suns.
I have abolished the whorehouses of France, Tangiers is the
           next to go.
My ambition is to be President despite the fact that I'm a
           Catholic.

America how can I write a holy litany in your silly mood?
I will continue like Henry Ford my strophes are as individual
           as his automobiles more so they're all different sexes.
America I will sell you strophes $2500 apiece $500 down on
           your old strophe
America free Tom Mooney
America save the Spanish Loyalists
America Sacco & Vanzetti must not die
America I am the Scottsboro boys.
America when I was seven Momma took me to Communist Cell
           meetings they sold us garbanzos a handful per ticket
           a ticket costs a nickel and the speeches were free
           everybody was angelic and sentimental about the
           workers it was all so sincere you have no idea what a
           good thing the party was in 1835 Scott Nearing was
           a grand old man a real mensch Mother Bloor made
           me cry I once saw Israel Amter plain. Everybody must
           have been a spy.
America you don't really want to go to war.
America it's them bad Russians.
Them Russians them Russians and them Chinamen. And them
           Russians.
The Russia wants to eat us alive. The Russia's power mad. She
           wants to take our cars from out our garages.

                                                    (6 9)

Her wants to grab Chicago. Her needs a Red Readers' Digest. Her wants our auto plants in Siberia. Him big bureaucracy running our fillingstations.
That no good. Ugh. Him make Indians learn read. Him need big black niggers. Hah. Her make us all work sixteen hours a day. Help.
America this is quite serious.
America this is the impression I get from looking in the television set.
America is this correct?
I'd better get right down to the job.
It's true I don't want to join the Army or turn lathes in precision parts factories, I'm nearsighted and psychopathic anyway.
America I'm putting my queer shoulder to the wheel.

PAUL GOODMAN

The Lordly Hudson

"Driver, what stream is it?" I asked, well knowing
it was our lordly Hudson hardly flowing,
"It is our lordly Hudson hardly flowing,"
he said, "under the green-grown cliffs."

Be still, heart! no one needs your passionate
suffrage to select this glory,
this is our lordly Hudson hardly flowing
under the green-grown cliffs.

"Driver! has this a peer in Europe or the East?"
"No no!" he said. Home! home!
be quiet, heart! this is our lordly Hudson
and has no peer in Europe or the East,

this is our lordly Hudson hardly flowing
under the green-grown cliffs
and has no peer in Europe or the East.
Be quiet, heart! home! home!

Poems of My Lambretta

1.

This pennant new
   my motorbike will fly:
a sea of icy blue
    and a pale blue sky
       and in the sky the wan
       yellow midnight sun,

Sally stitched for me
   of sturdy cloth
and silk embroidery
    to flaunt when forth
       I roar, so me all men
       may know by my emblem.

2.

My new license plate
is thirty zip six
orange and black
and cost me two bucks.

Castor and Pollux,
from cops preserve me
and all encounters
involving insurance.

Through lovely landscape
guide my wheels
and may my buddy-seat
carry friendly freight.

3.

Dirty and faded
   is the banner of my bike
and tattered in the winds
   of journey like

my self-esteem my soiled
   repute my faded hope.
The little motor but
   briskly roars me up

the hills and not half-way
   like some on Helicon.
Yet I recall a day
   she balked and stood there dumb.

It was no use to kick
   and swear at her. At her
own moment lightly she
   coughs, and off we roar!

on glad our windy way
   nowhere, going forty!
Flapping is my flag,
   faded torn and dirty,

and on the buddy-seat
   there rides Catullus dead
and speaks to me in gusts of shouts,
   I dare not turn my head.

4.

Oh we had the April evenings!
I had to tear myself away
a hasty kiss and on my way
past past the Cadillacs
that passed the Fords that passed the trucks,
I never had to jam the brakes
for I am a New Yorker bred,
the light is green all my road.
High in the forehead of the South
before me blazed in the lilac dusk

the Evening Star and I was drunk
on speed and the memory of your musk.
That was before I had the flat
and now the goddam clutch sticks
and you have gone to Bloomington.

Long Lines

The heavy glacier and the terrifying Alps
that simply I cannot, nor do I know the pass,
block me from Italy. As winter closes in,
just to survive I hole up in this hovel
with food that has no taste, no one to make love to
but fantasies and masturbating, sometimes sobbing
South! South! where white the torrent splashes down
past Lugano.
                    Yes, I know
I cannot move these mountains, but how did I stray
by cunningly bad choices up among these snows?
Are most of men as miserable but only some
enough communicative to declare how much?
Balked! balked! the dreary snowflakes do not cease
drifting past my window in the demi-dark.

April 1962

My countrymen have now become too base,
I give them up. I cannot speak with men
not my equals. I was an American,
where now to drag my days out and erase
this awful memory of the United States?
how can I work? I hired out my pen
to make my country practical, but I can
no longer serve these people, they are worthless.

"*Resign! resign!*" the word rings in my soul
—is it for me? or shall I make a sign
and picket the White House blindly in the rain,
or hold it up on Madison Avenue
until I vomit, or trudge to and fro
gloomily in front of the public school?

W. S. GRAHAM

Listen. Put on Morning

Listen. Put on morning.
Waken into falling light.
A man's imagining
Suddenly may inherit
The handclapping centuries
Of his one minute on earth.
And hear the virgin juries
Talk with his own breath
To the corner boys of his street.
And hear the Black Maria
Searching the town at night.
And hear the playropes caa
The sister Mary in.
And hear Willie and Davie
Among bracken of Narnain
Sing in a mist heavy
With myrtle and listeners.
And hear the higher town
Weep a petition of fears
At the poorhouse close upon
The public heartbeat.
And hear the children tig
And run with my own feet

Into the netting drag
Of a suiciding principle.
Listen. Put on lightbreak.
Waken into miracle.
The audience lies awake
Under the tenements
Under the sugar docks
Under the printed moments.
The centuries turn their locks
And open under the hill
Their inherited books and doors
All gathered to distil
Like happy berry pickers
One voice to talk to us.
Yes listen. It carries away
The second and the years
Till the heart's in a jacket of snow
And the head's in a helmet white
And the song sleeps to be wakened
By the morning ear bright.
Listen. Put on morning.
Waken into falling light.

HORACE GREGORY

The Beggar on the Beach

"I have not come here to talk;
I have come to sit; I have been transplanted
From the cornerstone of a First National Bank
On a windy street to root myself
In pebbles, shells, and sand;
It is my shadow and not my arm
That holds out its fingers in an empty glove
Which might so easily be mistaken for a hand.

(7 5)

My silence is
The unheard cries of those who swim
Where no raft follows, where sails, masts, funnels
Disappear up-ocean into a wave that travels
Eastward beyond the thin horizon line;
At my left shoulder there is a cloud
That gathers into a storm
On a beach-crowded Sunday afternoon—
The cloud my shadow's twin in the tide's swell
Which churns gold waters into lead and silver
At its will.

Tell me my riddle:
I am not a mirage, but a being in flesh
Born of a sea that has neither
Waves nor shore, nor moon, nor star:
That was my misfortune. Have you a better
Fortune? are you forever young, handsome, rich
In friends? poor in fear? happy in doubt?
Sad in nothing? hopeful in dark?
Is that what you are? Or do you burn
As my veins burn with ceaseless heat?
Whether you answer me or not,
Even at noon, the disguise I wear
Is the body and rags of legless Kronos
Before God walked the sky. Look at me and his shade
Turns boardwalk holidays into a mile
Of broken bottles and twisted iron
Seen through a gray window in the rain.

Give it your homage,
The shadow is always here. Now you may drop
Your money in my hat."

If It Offend Thee . . .

"I confess I would rather stand out for posterity in a hideous silhouette. . . . There happened to be the most innocent kind of party . . . at a
country house . . . at which there was a friend of my childhood that I
had not seen for years. . . . I invited the gentleman to step out on the
lawn, and there I beat him with a stick. . . . The next thing I remember
is returning late at night to my room. . . . There was a hard-coal fire
burning brightly . . . I plunged the left hand deep in the blaze . . .
and held it down with my right hand . . . I said to myself, 'This will
never do.'"

—M. A. DE WOLFE HOWE, *John Jay Chapman and His Letter*

'This will not do,' he said, and thrust his left hand into the coals
of the fire.
'This will not do . . . "if it offend thee" . . .' he kneeled to
thrust it deeper; he could not feel pain,
But felt the darkness fill the room behind him. He had awaked
from black sleep closed around him,
And saw his left hand shine in sin: it had struck down someone, perhaps an enemy, perhaps a friend.
' "If it offend thee . . ." ' That luminous face had disappeared,
even the smile; the face was like his own.
'This will not do,' he cried, and the charred fingers cracked between the coals;
The right hand held the left arm firm: it was strange enough
that he could feel no pain,
Only the darkness in the night behind him: somewhere the
enemy lay in the brushes, behind the night.
It had been a cold room, but now warm, the fire glowing. He
had slipped off his jacket before he slept
And heat leaped in the shadows on floor, on ceiling. The fire
opened its eyes into his eyes.
'This will not do . . .' unless he enter the fire to know the
greater heat, the rise, the fall of flames.
'If I go maimed,' he thought, 'I have struck it off; I shall not be
utterly dead, but living like
A living shade within the fire: damned, but alive in the heart
of the fire, to destroy the hand to make
Myself alive to live forever within the flames. There,' he withdrew the hand. It was nearly gone, but flesh remained;

(7 7)

It would not utterly disappear: 'This will not do,' he said. He
             had best go out. The room was cold and pain began.
He covered his left shoulder with a jacket; the hand was hidden,
             black as a snake, beneath it. He would ride—
If he could walk from the door down to the street—through
             elm-tossed Cambridge to an all-night clinic,
He would look like a soldier, drunk, in need of repair and a last
             straight drink. And the hand?
Even if struck off, what had been a hand would wear a glove.
             It would conceal a finger pointed at dark earth,
At earth, not fire, and it would say, 'This will not do.'

THOM GUNN

On the Move

"Man, you gotta Go."

The blue jay scuffling in the bushes follows
Some hidden purpose, and the gust of birds
That spurts across the field, the wheeling swallows,
Have nested in the trees and undergrowth.
Seeking their instinct, or their poise, or both,
One moves with an uncertain violence
Under the dust thrown by a baffled sense
Or the dull thunder of approximate words.

On motorcycles, up the road, they come:
Small, black, as flies hanging in heat, the Boys,
Until the distance throws them forth, their hum
Bulges to thunder held by calf and thigh.
In goggles, donned impersonality,
In gleaming jackets trophied with the dust,
They strap in doubt—by hiding it, robust—
And almost hear a meaning in their noise.

(78)

Exact conclusion of their hardiness
Has no shape yet, but from known whereabouts
They ride, direction where the tires press.
They scare a flight of birds across the field:
Much that is natural, to the will must yield.
Men manufacture both machine and soul,
And use what they imperfectly control
To dare a future from the taken routes.

It is a part solution, after all.
One is not necessarily discord
On earth; or damned because, half animal,
One lacks direct instinct, because one wakes
Afloat on movement that divides and breaks.
One joins the movement in a valueless world,
Choosing it, till, both hurler and the hurled,
One moves as well, always toward, toward.

A minute holds them, who have come to go:
The self-defined, astride the created will
They burst away; the towns they travel through
Are home for neither bird nor holiness,
For birds and saints complete their purposes.
At worst, one is in motion; and at best,
Reaching no absolute, in which to rest,
One is always nearer by not keeping still.

In Santa Maria Del Popolo

Waiting for when the sun an hour or less
Conveniently oblique makes visible
The painting on one wall of this recess
By Caravaggio, of the Roman School,
I see how shadow in the painting brims
With a real shadow, drowning all shapes out
But a dim horse's haunch and various limbs,
Until the very subject is in doubt.

(79)

But evening gives the act, beneath the horse
And one indifferent groom, I see him sprawl,
Foreshortened from the head, with hidden face,
Where he has fallen, Saul becoming Paul.
O wily painter, limiting the scene
From a cacophony of dusty forms
To the one convulsion, what is it you mean
In that wide gesture of the lifting arms?

No Ananias croons a mystery yet,
Casting the pain out under name of sin.
The painter saw what was, an alternate
Candor and secrecy inside the skin.
He painted, elsewhere, that firm insolent
Young whore in Venus' clothes, those pudgy cheats,
Those sharpers; and was strangled, as things went,
For money, by one such picked off the streets.

RAMON   GUTHRIE

The Clown: He Dances
in the Clearing by Night

He took his wig off, with his sleeve
wiped painted snigger from his face
and did a dance you'd not believe . . .
with easy-jointed limpid pace
wove through such figures as the eye
could scarcely follow, whistling slow
a tune of scant variety
like whispers on a piccolo.

The Tyger in his forest stared,
chin sunk upon his powered paws
while pirouette and caper dared
the awesome sinews of the Laws

his stripèd humors improvise—
Immutabilities laid down
by conclaves of eternities—
revoked an instant by the Clown.

He danced the twittering of quails
and dolphins' pleasure in the sea
and planets screaming on their rails
of finely drawn infinity.
Then naked, having cast aside
motley of Time and Space and Number,
he glided silent through the wide
vistas of the Tyger's slumber.

Postlude: for Goya

A bloody day subsided: the volcano's lips
cool to slag, its glow a tracery
faint against the sky. (Oh, there is still
a sky) How different this calm from peace.
We are too shattered now to count our losses.
What is there left but loss? Who still can hope
that because we fought, others in time will fight,
because we were broken that earth still holds
some traces of a destiny?

We are alone to-night, each of us alone,
before and after a storm, breathing in a lull,
caught in a bight of ashy slackness.
A broad lightning painted on the sky shows livid
two skinned bulls, motionless, backed off
from goring one another. We crouch
behind a knoll of pumice and the dry clouds lie
so near above us we could reach a hand
almost to touch them. There is dust in our mouths.
Beads of useless power
exude like gum from the earth and sounds
are sucked from our lips by the silence. At our feet
the bones of a buzzard lie beside
the shadowy fox's bones that stalked it.

You stare at a dry hollow and your lips
peel back from your teeth
and your shoulders mean laughter,
remembering it lately was a brook.
(We must not shrink to gauge our madness,
the heat-sprung brain and fingers brittle as
scorched ivory, eyes with certain visions baked
into them.) This is not an end,
only an interlude: after a while
we will creep forth and search among the crevices
for seeds and cover them with dust
and try for tears to quicken them.
Remember only this is not an end.
We have won if we can believe
that this is not an end.

To and on Other Intellectual Poets on Reading That the U.S.A.F. Had Sent a Team of Scientists to Africa to Learn Why Giraffes Do Not Black Out

"Ses ailes de géant l'empêchent de marcher."

—BAUDELAIRE

You an' me, bister, been giraffes—
equipped with them outside
terrential necks which when it comes
to trees can munch the tops of
and when it comes to telegraph lines
just snag right through them
But when it is merely a matter of browsing grass
has to can't
except they prop their
legs apart like a hasty whore
hoping to wind up work in time to catch
the 11:54
to her home in the Ramapos
or a pair of calipers attempting to describe
a circle too wide for itself to span
without spraining its furcal ligaments

And even how we keep
from blacking out
Science is still
scratching its pretty head about.

DONALD HALL

Wells

I lived in a dry well
under the rank grass of a meadow.

A white ladder leaned out of it
but I was afraid of the sounds

of animals grazing.
I crouched by the wall ten years

until the circle of a woman's darkness
moved over mine like a mouth.

The ladder broke out in leaves
and fruit hung from the branches.

I climbed to the meadow grass.
I drink from the well of cattle.

The Snow

Snow is in the oak.
Behind the thick, whitening
air which the wind drives,
the weight of the sun
presses the snow
on the pane of my window.

(8 3)

I remember snows and my walking
through their first fall in cities,
asleep or drunk
with the slow, desperate falling.
The snow blurs in my eyes
with other snows.

Snow is what must
come down, even if it struggles
to stay in the air with the strength
of the wind. Like an old man,
whatever I touch I turn
to the story of death.

Snow is what fills
the oak, and what covers
the grass and the bare garden.
Snow is what reverses
the sidewalk and the lawn
into the substance of whiteness.

So the watcher sleeps himself
back to the baby's eyes.
The tree, the breast, and the floor
are limbs of him, and from
his eyes he extends a skin
which grows over the world.

The baby is what must
have fallen, like snow. He resisted,
the way the old man
struggles inside the airy tent
to keep on breathing.
Birth is the fear of death

but snow is what melts.
I cannot open the door
to the cycles of water.
The sun has withdrawn itself
and the snow keeps falling,
and something will always be falling.

(8 4)

MICHAEL HAMBURGER

A Child Accepts

"Later," his mother said; and still those little hands
Clawed air to clutch the object of their need,
Abandoned as birds to winds or fishes to tide,
Pure time that is timeless, time untenanted.

"Later," she said; and the word was cold with death,
Opposing space to his time, intersecting his will.
He summoned the cry of a wounded animal,
Mindless Adam whose world lies crushed by the Fall,

But suddenly mended his face and far from tears
Grew radiant, relaxed, letting his hands drop down.
"Later," he sang, and was human, fallen again,
Received into mind, his dubious, his true demesne.

"Later," he played with the word, and later will envy
The freedom of birds and fishes for ever lost,
When, migrant in mind whom wind and water resist,
Here he must winter in body, bound to the coast;

Or, not all his "laters" past, perhaps he'll know
That the last releases: reversed, his needs will throng
Homewards to nest in his head and breed among
Those hidden rocks that wrecked him into song.

Homage to the Weather

A tide, high tide of golden air.

Where, till this moment, were the bees?
And when no hum made for the honeysuckle,
Fumbled,
Became a body,

Clung and drank,
Spindrift, disowned, the petals hung,
And wait, let go was what the summer meant.

A corner of the garden, ivy on broken slats,
A branch with orange puffs: buddleia globosa.
Between two gusts a flood of golden air,
Mere hush, perhaps, abeyance—but the bees
Clinging and drinking.

Walls they brought with them: black courtyard in Paris,
A bit of marble, tumbled, dust on leaves,
A goldfish pond, the traffic not remote,
Audible, yet excluded;
Flowering tree or shrub in any weathered city,
Walls to contain a quietness, a quiver,
Fulfilment of the year, bees to be stilled.

Between two gusts, cold waves, the golden tide.

Security

1

So he's got there at last, been received as a partner—
In a firm going bankrupt;
Found the right place (walled garden), arranged for a mort-
          gage—
But they're pulling the house down
To make room for traffic.

Worse winds are rising. He takes out new policies
For his furniture, for his life,
At a higher premium
Against more limited risks.

2

Who can face the winds, till the panes crack in their frames?
And if a man faced them, what in the end could he do
But look for shelter like all the rest?
The winds too are afraid, and blow from fear.

3

I hear my children at play
And recall that one branch of the elm-tree looks dead;
Also that twenty years ago now I could have been parchment
Cured and stretched for a lampshade,
Who now have children, a lampshade
And the fear of those winds.

I saw off the elm-tree branch
To find that the wood was sound;
Mend the fences yet again,
Knowing they'll keep out no one,
Let alone the winds.
For still my children play,
And shall tomorrow, if the weather holds.

Omens

1

The year opens with frozen pipes,
Roads impassable, cars immovable,
Letter delivery slow;
But smallpox from Pakistan
Carried fast from Yorkshire to Surrey,
And no lack of news:
In the Andes a landslide
That buried a town;
In Dalmatia, earthquakes;
Bush fires around Melbourne,
Cooking wallabies, koala bears.
In the Congo, another rebellion;
In Algeria, random murders on either side;
Paris a playground for thugs.

2

The milk our children drink may or may not be poisoned
By last year's fall-out, no longer part of the news.
Our earth may be shrinking, expanding
But was found to contain great cracks
That will doubtless widen even without our help.

(8 7)

3

Amid such omens
How do we dare to live?
Brashly building, begetting
For a town besieged,
Crumbling, patched again, crumbling
And undermined?

4

Deeper I gulp cold air that not too suddenly kills,
Greedily drink with my eyes the winter sunshine and clouds,
The old white horse in the meadow
Green again after snow.

Next year I shall see no meadow, no horse.

ANTHONY HECHT

Drinking Song

A toast to that lady over the fireplace
Who wears a snood of pearls. Her eyes are turned
Away from the posterity that loosed
Drunken invaders to the living room,
Toppled the convent bell-tower, and burned
The sniper-ridden outhouses. The face
Of Beatrice d'Este, reproduced
In color, offers a profile to this dark,
Hand-carved interior. High German gloom
Flinches before our boots upon the desk
Where the *Ortsgruppenführer* used to park
His sovereign person. Not a week ago
The women of this house went down among
The stacked-up kindling wood, the picturesque,

Darkening etchings of Vesuvius,
Piled mattresses upon themselves, and shook,
And prayed to God in their guttural native tongue
For mercy, forgiveness, and the death of us.

We are indeed diminished.
                              We are twelve.
But have recaptured a sufficiency
Of France's cognac; and it shall be well,
Given sufficient time, if we can down
Half of it, being as we are, reduced.
Five dead in the pasture, yet they loom
As thirstily as ever. Are recalled
By daring wagers to this living room:
I'll be around to leak over your grave."

And *Durendal,* my only *Durendal,*
Thou hast preserved me better than a sword;
Rest in the enemy umbrella stand
While that I measure out another drink.
I am beholden to thee, by this hand,
This measuring hand. We are beholden all.

GEOFFREY HILL

Doctor Faustus

> For it must needs be that offences come; but
> woe to that man by whom the offence cometh.

I THE EMPEROR'S CLOTHES

A way of many ways: a god
Spirals in the pure steam of blood.
And gods—as men—rise from shut tombs
To a disturbance of small drums;

(8 9)

Immaculate plumage of the swan
The common wear. There is no-one
Afraid or overheard, no loud
Voice (though innocently loud).

II THE HARPIES

Having stood hungrily apart
From the gods' politic banquet,
Of all possible false gods
I fall to these gristled shades

That show everything, without lust;
And stumble upon their dead feast
By the torn *Warning to Bathers*
By the torn waters.

III ANOTHER PART OF THE FABLE

The innocents have not flown;
Too legendary, they laugh;
The lewd uproarious wolf
Brings their house down.

A beast is slain, a beast thrives.
Fat blood squeaks on the sand.
A blinded god believes
That he is not blind.

JOHN HOLLOWAY

Family Poem

Now dis-band all the bands of kin:
Not even the falcon's glaring eye
Can trace kin out in jealousy
And hate and spite and every sin

(9 0)

That tetters the bewildered spirit
That ails and dies like flesh its twin,
Turns bright with rot: unless love fire it.

Nor can love fire it, among those
Who are poor, blind, ugly, old, frustrated,
Quite stuck for why they bred or mated:
Like a lush hot-house flower, it grows
By art; and only gentleness
Can spread its petals till it glows.
Not acid soil of sharp distress.

So, like a scientist, I strain
And probe all day, until I breed
A mountain kind, rich with a seed
Immune to cold and dark and rain,
Kindling the black rock and the mud
In tides of red: a tenuous weed,
But one that takes no food save blood.

The Brothers

South, in the town, the sun had spread
All day flame-warm. Their lives had been
Colourful and noisy as a fair
For a long time. Northward, instead,
A wind-cleared sky ranged iron green.
Frost gripped the hill. The copse lay bare.

Yet, slowly, slowly, they all
(By the sharp east or gentle west)
Bowed to the image, and returned.
That distant place was radical.
Going there was the acid test.
But they forgot how acid burned.

The light grew cold. The journey spread
Itself out strangely. Space became
A conjurer's trick, and multiplied:

(9 1)

Because the living and the dead
Possess (though they may share one name)
No common ground, however wide.

And spread too, since the will that drove
Them, jarred against their course: like brakes,
Harsher and harsher as they neared,
For now they saw this one could prove
Unmendable among mistakes.
Then small as life the croft appeared.

There on the brown dew-budded turf
Greedy as crows all three they stood.
They saw the copse, the five hay-stacks,
The hill; heard the ice wind, the surf.
Found no sweet impossible food.
Gazed at each other. Turned their backs.

KATHERINE HOSKINS

Nuit Blanche

Blind for the lamp she's smashed and the riving tears,
She who, one by one,
Fetches up griefs like stones
The quiet years have mossed
And heaves them far far off;
Riven, shriven wakes her
To passion's dank black crater
And her griefs dead-ahead, fallow for the light-foot years.

GRAHAM HOUGH

Dark Corner

If ever the sun had thought to pass this way
It would have scaled the last paint from the walls,
Rotted the garbage to a decent mould
And baked the stinking damp to feathery dust.

If ever the wind swept through it would have puffed
The dust about the sky to paint a sunset,
Hidden the stench, rank garlic for a stew,
In the rough tawny savour of the city.

If ever the rain had dropped to drench these stones
The gutter would have swilled down to the sea
Excrement, soaking rags and moulted hair,
And sunk the filthy cargo in the blue—

So salt, so deep, it could have drowned the lot,
Scoured, bleached and scattered all the standing dregs,
Bred from their atoms corals, long-spined shells,
Urchins, thready weeds and wrack, slow pearls,
To branch and glimmer in the living flood.

TED HUGHES

Hawk Roosting

I sit in the top of the wood, my eyes closed.
Inaction, no falsifying dream
Between my hooked head and hooked feet:
Or in sleep rehearse perfect kills and eat.

(9 3)

The convenience of the high trees!
The air's buoyancy and the sun's ray
Are of advantage to me;
And the earth's face upward for my inspection.

My feet are locked upon the rough bark.
It took the whole of Creation
To produce my foot, my each feather:
Now I hold Creation in my foot

Or fly up, and revolve it all slowly—
I kill where I please because it is all mine.
There is no sophistry in my body:
My manners are tearing off heads—

The allotment of death.
For the one path of my flight is direct
Through the bones of the living.
No arguments assert my right:

The sun is behind me.
Nothing has changed since I began.
My eye has permitted no change.
I am going to keep things like this.

November

The month of the drowned dog. After long rain the land
Was sodden as the bed of an ancient lake,
Treed with iron and birdless. In the sunk lane
The ditch—a seep silent all summer—

Made brown foam with a big voice: that, and my boots
On the lane's scrubbed stones, in the gulleyed leaves,
Against the hill's hanging silence;
Mist silvering the droplets on the bare thorns

Slower than the change of daylight.
In a let of the ditch a tramp was bundled asleep:

Face tucked down into beard, drawn in
Under its hair like a hedgehog's. I took him for dead,

But his stillness separated from the death
Of the rotting grass and the ground. A wind chilled,
And a fresh comfort tightened through him,
Each hand stuffed deeper into the other sleeve.

His ankles, bound with sacking and hairy band,
Rubbed each other, resettling. The wind hardened;
A puff shook a glittering from the thorns,
And again the rains' dragging grey columns

Smudged the farms. In a moment
The fields were jumping and smoking; the thorns
Quivered, riddled with the glassy verticals.
I stayed on under the welding cold

Watching the tramp's face glisten and the drops on his coat
Flash and darken. I thought what strong trust
Slept in him—as the trickling furrows slept,
And the thorn-roots in their grip on darkness;

And the buried stones, taking the weight of winter;
The hill where the hare crouched with clenched teeth.
Rain plastered the land till it was shining
Like hammered lead, and I ran, and in the rushing wood

Shuttered by a black oak leaned.
The keeper's gibbet had owls and hawks
By the neck, weasels, a gang of cats, crows:
Some, stiff, weightless, twirled like dry bark bits

In the drilling rain. Some still had their shape,
Had their pride with it; hung, chins on chests,
Patient to outwait these worst days that beat
Their crowns bare and dripped from their feet.

Pike

Pike, three inches long, perfect
Pike in all parts, green tigering the gold.

(9 5)

Killers from the egg: the malevolent aged grin.
They dance on the surface among the flies.

Or move, stunned by their own grandeur,
Over a bed of emerald, silhouette
Of submarine delicacy and horror.
A hundred feet long in their world.

In ponds, under the heat-struck lily pads—
Gloom of their stillness:
Logged on last year's black leaves, watching upwards.
Or hung in an amber cavern of weeds

The jaws' hooked clamp and fangs
Not to be changed at this date;
A life subdued to its instrument;
The gills kneading quietly, and the pectorals.

Three we kept behind glass,
Jungled in weed: three inches, four,
And four and a half: fed fry to them—
Suddenly there were two. Finally one

With a sag belly and the grin it was born with.
And indeed they spare nobody.
Two, six pounds each, over two feet long,
High and dry and dead in the willow-herb—

One jammed past its gills down the other's gullet:
The outside eye stared: as a vice locks—
The same iron in this eye
Though its film shrank in death.

A pond I fished, fifty yards across,
Whose lilies and muscular tench
Had outlasted every visible stone
Of the monastery that planted them—

Stilled legendary depth:
It was as deep as England. It held
Pike too immense to stir, so immense and old
That past nightfall I dared not cast

But silently cast and fished
With the hair frozen on my head
For what might move, for what eye might move.
The still splashes on the dark pond,

Owls hushing the floating woods
Frail on my ear against the dream
Darkness beneath night's darkness had freed,
That rose slowly towards me, watching.

Lupercalia

1

The dog loved its churlish life,
Scraps, thefts. Its declined blood
An anarchy of mindless pride.
Nobody's pet, but good enough

To double with a bitch as poor.
It had bitten ears and little stone eyes,
A mouth like an incinerator.
It held man's reasonable ways

Between its teeth. Received death
Closed eyes and grinning mouth.

2

This woman's as from death's touch: a surviving
Barrenness: she abides; perfect,
But flung from the wheel of the living,
The past killed in her, the future plucked out.

The dead are indifferent underground.
Little the live may learn from them—
A sort of hair and bone wisdom,
A worn witchcraft accoutrement

Of proverbs. Now the brute's quick
Be tinder: Old spark of the blood-heat
And not death's touch engross her bed,
Though that has stripped her stark indeed.

3

Goats, black, not angels, but
Bellies round as filled wine-skins
Slung under carcase bones.
Yet that's no brute light

And no merely mountain light—
Their eyes' golden element.
Rustle of their dry hooves, dry patter,
Wind in the oak-leaves; and their bent

Horns, stamp, sudden reared stare
Startle women. Spirit of the ivy,
Stink of goat, of a rank thriving,
O mountain listener.

4

Over sand that the sun's burned out
Thudding feet of the powerful,
Their oiled bodies brass-bright
In a drift of dust. The earth's crammed full,

Its baked red bellying to the sky's
Electric blue. Their attitudes—
A theorem of flung effort, blades:
Nothing mortal falters their poise

Though wet with blood: the dog has blessed
Their fury. Fresh thongs of goat-skin
In their hands they go bounding past,
And deliberate welts have snatched her in

To the figure of racers. Maker of the world,
Hurrying the lit ghost of man
Age to age while the body hold,
Touch this frozen one.

An Otter

Underwater eyes, an eel's
Oil of water body, neither fish nor beast is the otter:
Four-legged yet water-gifted, to outfish fish;
With webbed feet and long ruddering tail
And a round head like an old tomcat.

Brings the legend of himself
From before wars or burials, in spite of hounds and vermin-
poles;
Does not take root like the badger. Wanders, cries;
Gallops along land he no longer belongs to;
Re-enters the water by melting.

Of neither water nor land. Seeking
Some world lost when first he dived, that he cannot come at
since,
Takes his changed body into the holes of lakes;
As if blind, cleaves the stream's push till he licks
The pebbles of the source; from sea

To sea crosses in three nights
Like a king in hiding. Crying to the old shape of the starlit land,
Over sunken farms where the bats go round,
Without answer. Till light and birdsong come
Walloping up roads with the milk wagon.

II

The hunt's lost him. Pads on mud,
Among sedges, nostrils a surface bead,
The otter remains, hours. The air,
Circling the globe, tainted and necessary,

Mingling tobacco-smoke, hounds and parsley,
Comes carefully to the sunk lungs.
So the self under the eye lies,
Attendant and withdrawn. The otter belongs

In double robbery and concealment—
From water that nourishes and drowns, and from land

That gave him his length and the mouth of the hound.
He keeps fat in the limpid integument

Reflections live on. The heart beats thick,
Big trout muscle out of the dead cold;
Blood is the belly of logic; he will lick
The fishbone bare. And can take stolen hold

On a bitch otter in a field full
Of nervous horses, but linger nowhere.
Yanked above hounds, reverts to nothing at all,
To this long pelt over the back of a chair.

RANDALL JARRELL

The Death of the Ball Turret Gunner

From my mother's sleep I fell into the State,
And I hunched in its belly till my wet fur froze.
Six miles from earth, loosed from its dream of life,
I woke to black flak and the nightmare fighters.
When I died they washed me out of the turret with a hose.

A Camp in the Prussian Forest

I walked beside the prisoners to the road.
Load on puffed load,
Their corpses stacked like sodden wood,
Lie barred or galled with blood

(1 0 0)

By the charred warehouse. No one comes today
In the old way
To knock the fillings from their teeth;
The dark, coned, common wreath

Is plaited for their grave—a kind of grief.
The living leaf
Clings to the planted profitable
Pine if it is able;

The boughs sigh, mile on green, calm, breathing mile,
From this dead file
The planners ruled for them. . . . One year
They sent a million here:

Here men were drunk like water, burnt like wood.
The fat of good
And evil, the breast's star of hope
Were rendered into soap.

I paint the star I sawed from yellow pine—
And plant the sign
In soil that does not yet refuse
Its usual Jews

Their first asylum. But the white, dwarfed star—
This dead white star—
Hides nothing, pays for nothing; smoke
Fouls it, a yellow joke,

The needles of the wreath are chalked with ash,
A filmy trash
Litters the black woods with the death
Of men; and one last breath

Curls from the monstrous chimney. . . . I laugh aloud
Again and again;
The star laughs from its rotting shroud
Of flesh. O star of men!

The Black Swan

When the swans turned my sister into a swan
   I would go to the lake, at night, from milking:
The sun would look out through the reeds like a swan,
   A swan's red beak; and the beak would open
And inside there was darkness, the stars and the moon.

Out on the lake a girl would laugh.
   "Sister, here is your porridge, sister,"
I would call; and the reeds would whisper,
   "Go to sleep, go to sleep, little swan."
My legs were all hard and webbed, and the silky

Hairs of my wings sank away like stars
   In the ripples that ran in and out of the reeds:
I heard through the lap and hiss of water
   Someone's "Sister . . . sister," far away on the shore,
And then as I opened my beak to answer

I heard my harsh laugh go out to the shore
   And saw—saw at last, swimming up from the green
Low mounds of the lake, the white stone swans:
   The white, named swans . . . "It is all a dream,"
I whispered, and reached from the down of the pallet

To the lap and hiss of the floor.
   And "Sleep, little sister," the swans all sang
From the moon and stars and frogs of the floor.
   But the swan my sister called, "Sleep at last, little sister,"
And stroked all night, with a black wing, my wings.

The Woman at the Washington Zoo

The saris go by me from the embassies.

Cloth from the moon. Cloth from another planet.
They look back at the leopard like the leopard.

And I. . . .
                    this print of mine, that has kept its color
Alive through so many cleanings; this dull null
Navy I wear to work, and wear from work, and so
To my bed, so to my grave, with no
Complaints, no comment: neither from my chief,
The Deputy Chief Assistant, nor his chief—
Only I complain. . . . this serviceable
Body that no sunlight dyes, no hand suffuses
But, dome-shadowed, withering among columns,
Wavy beneath fountains—small, far-off, shining
In the eyes of animals, those beings trapped
As I am trapped but not, themselves, the trap,
Aging, but without knowledge of their age,
Kept safe here, knowing not of death, for death—
Oh, bars of my own body, open, open!

The world goes by my cage and never sees me.
And there come not to me, as come to these,
The wild beasts, sparrows pecking the llamas' grain,
Pigeons settling on the bears' bread, buzzards
Tearing the meat the flies have clouded. . . .
                                        Vulture,
When you come for the white rat that the foxes left,
Take off the red helmet of your head, the black
Wings that had shadowed me, and step to me as man:
The wild brother at whose feet the white wolves fawn,
To whose hand of power the great lioness
Stalks, purring. . . .
                    You know what I was,
You see what I am: change me, change me!

A Death

"His face shone" she said,
"Three days I had him in my house,
Three days before they took him from his bed,
And never have I felt so close."

"Always alive he was
A little drawn away from me.
Looks are opaque when living and his face
Seemed hiding something, carefully."

"But those three days before
They took his body out, I used to go
And talk to him. That shining from him bore
No secrets. Living, he never looked or answered so."

Sceptic I listened, then
Noted what peace she seemed to have,
How tenderly she put flowers on his grave
But not as if he might return again
Or shine or seem quite close:
Rather to please us were the flowers she gave.

Song for a Departure

Could you indeed come lightly
Leaving no mark at all
Even of footsteps, briefly
Visit not change the air
Of this or the other room,
Have quick words with us yet be
Calm and unhurried here?

So that we should not need—
When you departed lightly
Even as swift as coming
Letting no shadow fall—
Changes, surrenders, fear,
Speeches grave to the last,
But feel no loss at all?

Lightest things in the mind
Go deep at last and can never
Be planned or weighed or lightly
Considered or set apart.
Then come like a great procession,
Touch hours with drums and flutes:
Fill all the rooms of our houses
And haunt them when you depart.

LEROI JONES

Way Out West

FOR GARY SNYDER

As simple an act
as opening the eyes. Merely
coming into things by degrees.

Morning: some tear is broken
on the wooden stairs
of my lady's eyes. Profusions
of green. The leaves. Their
constant prehensions. Like old
junkies on Sheridan Square, eyes
cold and round. There is a song
Nat Cole sings . . . This city
& the intricate disorder
of the seasons.

Unable to mention
something as abstract as time.

Even so, (bowing low in thick
smoke from cheap incense; all
kinds of questions filling the mouth,
till you suffocate & fall dead
to opulent carpet.) Even so,

shadows will creep over your flesh
& hide your disorder, your lies.

There are unattractive wild ferns
outside the window
where the cats hide. They yowl
from there at nights. In heat
& bleeding on my tulips.

Steel bells, like the evil
unwashed Sphinx, towing in the twilight.
Childless old murderers, for centuries
with musty eyes.

I am distressed. Thinking
of the seasons, how they pass,
how I pass, my very youth, the
ripe sweet of my life; drained off . . .

Like giant rhesus monkeys;
picking their skulls,
with ingenious cruelty
sucking out the brains.

No use for beauty
collapsed, with moldy breath
done in. Insidious weight
of cankered dreams. Tiresias'
weathered cock.

(1 0 6)

Walking into the sea, shells
caught in the hair. Coarse
waves tearing the tongue.

Closing the eyes. As
simply an act. You float

PATRICK KAVANAGH

If Ever You Go to Dublin Town

If ever you go to Dublin town
In a hundred years or so
Inquire for me in Baggot Street
And what I was like to know.
O he was a queer one
Fol dol the di do,
He was a queer one
I tell you.

My great-grandmother knew him well,
He asked her to come and call
On him in his flat and she giggled at the thought
Of a young girl's lovely fall.
O he was dangerous
Fol dol the di do,
He was dangerous
I tell you.

On Pembroke Road look out for my ghost
Dishevelled with shoes untied,
Playing through the railings with little children
Whose children have long since died.
O he was a nice man
Fol dol the di do,
He was a nice man
I tell you.

Go into a pub and listen well
If my voice still echoes there,
Ask the men what their grandsires thought
And tell them to answer fair.
O he was eccentric
Fol dol the di do,
He was eccentric
I tell you.

He had the knack of making men feel
As small as they really were
Which meant as great as God had made them
But as males they disliked his air.
O he was a proud one
Fol dol the di do,
He was a proud one
I tell you.

If ever you go to Dublin town
In a hundred years or so
Sniff for my personality,
Is it vanity's vapour now?
O he was a vain one
Fol dol the di do,
He was a vain one
I tell you.

I saw his name with a hundred others
In a book in the library,
It said he had never fully achieved
His potentiality.
O he was slothful
Fol dol the di do,
He was slothful
I tell you.

He knew that posterity has no use
For anything but the soul,
The lines that speak the passionate heart,
The spirit that lives alone.
O he was a lone one
Fol dol the di do,
Yet he lived happily
I tell you.

(1 0 8)

FROM *Father Mat*

I

                    In a meadow
Beside the chapel three boys were playing football.
At the forge door an old man was leaning
Viewing a hunter-hoe. A man could hear
If he listened to the breeze the fall of wings—
How wistfully the sin-birds come home!

It was Confession Saturday, the first
Saturday in May; the May Devotions
Were spread like leaves to quieten
The excited armies of conscience.
The knife of penance fell so like a blade
Of grass that no one was afraid.

Father Mat came slowly walking, stopping to
Stare through gaps at ancient Ireland sweeping
In again with all its unbaptized beauty:
The calm evening,
The whitethorn blossoms,
The smell from ditches that were not Christian.
The dancer that dances in the hearts of men cried:
Look! I have shown this to you before—
The rags of living surprised
The joy in things you cannot forget.

His heavy hat was square upon his head,
Like a Christian Brother's;
His eyes were an old man's watery eyes,
Out of his flat nose grew spiky hairs.
He was a part of the place,
Natural as a round stone in a grass field;
He could walk through a cattle fair
And the people would only notice his odd spirit there.

His curate passed on a bicycle—
He had the haughty intellectual look
Of the man who never reads in brook or book;
A man designed
To wear a mitre,

(*1 0 9*)

To sit on committees—
For will grows strongest in the emptiest mind.

The old priest saw him pass
And, seeing, saw
Himself a mediaeval ghost.
Ahead of him went Power,
One who was not afraid when the sun opened a flower,
Who was never astonished
At a stick carried down a stream
Or at the undying difference in the corner of a field.

GALWAY KINNELL

Duck-Chasing

I spied a very small brown duck
Riding the swells of the sea
Like a rocking-chair. "Little duck!"
I cried. It paddled away,
I paddled after it. When it dived,
Down I dived: too smoky was the sea,
We were lost. It surfaced
In the west, I torpedoed west
And when it dived I dived,
And we were lost and lost and lost
In the slant smoke of the sea.
When I came floating up on it
From the side, like a deadman,
And yelled suddenly, it took off,
It skimmed the swells as it ascended,
Brown wings burning and flashing
In the sun as the sea rose over
Burned and flashed underneath it.
I did not see the little duck again.
Duck-chasing is a game like any game.
When it is over it is all over.

FROM *The Avenue Bearing the Initial of Christ into the New World*

FOR GAIL

Was diese kleine Gasse doch für ein Reich an sich war . . .

2

In sunlight on the Avenue
The Jew rocks along in a black fur shtraimel,
Black robe, black knickers, black knee-stockings,
Black shoes. His beard like a sod-bottom
Hides the place where he wears no tie.
A dozen children troop after him, barbels flying,
In skullcaps. They are Reuben, Simeon, Levi, Judah, Issachar,
        Zebulun, Benjamin, Dan, Naphtali, Gad, Asher.
With the help of the Lord they will one day become
Courtiers, thugs, rulers, rabbis, asses, adders, wrestlers, bakers,
        poets, cartpushers, infantrymen.

The old man is sad-faced. He is near burial
And one son is missing. The women who bore him sons
And are past bearing, mourn for the son
And for the father, wondering if the man will go down
Into the grave of a son mourning, or if at the last
The son will put his hands on the eyes of his father.

The old man wades towards his last hour.
On 5th Street, between Avenues A and B,
In sunshine, in his private cloud, Bunko Certified Embalmer,
Cigar in his mouth, nose to the wind, leans
At the doorway of Bunko's Funeral Home & Parlour,
Glancing west towards the Ukrainians, eastward idly
Where the Jew rocks towards his last hour.
Sons, grandsons at his heel, the old man
Confronts the sun. He does not feel its rays
Through his beard, he does not understand
Fruits and vegetables live by the sun.
Like his children he is sallow-faced, he sees
A blinding signal in the sky, he smiles.

Bury me not Bunko damned Catholic I pray you in Egypt.

                                 (1 1 1)

From the Station House
Under demolishment on Houston
To the Power Station on 14th,
Jews, Negroes, Puerto Ricans
Walk in the spring sunlight.

The Downtown Talmud Torah
Blosztein's Cutrate Bakery
Areceba Panataria Hispano
Peanuts Dried Fruit Nuts & Canned Goods
Productos Tropicales
Appetizing Herring Candies Nuts
Nathan Kugler Chicken Store Fresh Killed Daily
Little Rose Restaurant
Rubinstein the Hatter Mens Boys Hats Caps Furnishings
J. Herrmann Dealer in All Kinds of Bottles
Natural Bloom Cigars
Blony Bubblegum
Mueren las Cucarachas Super Potente Garantizada de Matar las
        Cucarachas mas Resistentes
Wenig מצבות
G. Schnee Stairbuilder
Everyouth la Original Loción Eterna Juventud Satisfacción
        Dinero Devuelto
Happy Days Bar & Grill

Through dust-stained windows over storefronts
Curtains drawn aside, onto the Avenue
Thronged with Puerto Ricans, Negroes, Jews,
Baby carriages stuffed with groceries and babies,
The old women peer, blessed damozels
Sitting up there young forever in the cockroached rooms,
Eating fresh-killed chicken, productos tropicales,
Appetizing herring, canned goods, nuts;
They puff out smoke from Natural Bloom cigars
And one day they puff like Blony Bubblegum.
Across the square skies with faces in them
Pigeons skid, crashing into the brick.
From a rooftop a boy fishes at the sky,
Around him a flock of pigeons fountains,

(*1 1* 2)

Blown down and swirling up again, seeking the sky.
From a skyview of the city they must seem
A whirlwind on the desert seeking itself;
Here they break from the rims of the buildings
Without rank in the blue military cemetery sky.
A red kite wriggles like a tadpole
Into the sky beyond them, crosses
The sun, lays bare its own crossed skeleton.

To fly from this place—to roll
On some bubbly blacktop in the summer,
To run under the rain of pigeon plumes, to be
Tarred, and feathered with birdshit, Icarus,

In Kugler's glass headdown dangling by yellow legs.

6

In the pushcart market, on Sunday,
A crate of lemons discharges light like a battery.
Icicle-shaped carrots that through black soil
Wove away lie like flames in the sun.
Onions with their shirts ripped seek sunlight
On green skins. The sun beats
On beets dirty as boulders in cowfields,
On turnips pinched and gibbous
From budging rocks, on embery sweets,
Peanut-shaped Idahos, shore-pebble Long Islands and Maines,
On horseradishes still growing weeds on the flat ends,
Cabbages lying about like sea-green brains
The skulls have been shucked from,
On tomatoes, undented plum-tomatoes, alligator-skinned
Cucumbers, that float pickled
In the wooden tubs of green skim milk—

Sky-flowers, dirt-flowers, underdirt-flowers,
Those that climbed for the sun in their lives
And those that wormed away—equally uprooted,
Maimed, lopped, shucked, and misaimed.

In the market in Damascus a goat
Came to a stall where twelve goatheads
Were lined up for sale. It sniffed them

One by one. Finally thirteen goats started
Smiling in their faintly sardonic way.

A crone buys a pickle from a crone,
It is wrapped in the *Mirror*,
At home she will open the wrapping, stained,
And stare and stare and stare at it.
And the cucumbers, and the melons,
And the leeks, and the onions, and the garlic.

11

The fishmarket closed, the fishes gone into flesh.
The smelts draped on each other, fat with roe,
The marble cod hacked into chunks on the counter,
Butterfishes mouths still open, still trying to eat,
Porgies with receding jaws hinged apart
In a grimace of dejection, as if like cows
They had died under the sledgehammer, perches
In grass-green armor, spotted squeteagues
In the melting ice meek-faced and croaking no more,
Except in the plip plop plip plip in the bucket,
Mud-eating mullets buried in crushed ice,
Tilefishes with scales like chickenfat,
Spanish mackerels, buttercups on the flanks,
Pot-bellied pikes, two-tone flounders
After the long contortion of pushing both eyes
To the brown side that they might look up,
Brown side down, like a mass laying-on of hands,
Or the oath-taking of an army.

The only things alive are the carp
That drift in the black tank in the rear,
Kept living for the usual reason, that they have not died,
And perhaps because the last meal was garbage and they might
        begin stinking
On dying, before the customer was halfway home.
They nudge each other, to be netted,
The sweet flesh to be lifted thrashing in the air,
To be slugged, and then to keep on living
While they are opened on the counter.
Fishes do not die exactly, it is more
That they go out of themselves, the visible part

(1 1 4)

Remains the same, there is little pallor,
Only the cataracted eyes which have not shut ever
Must look through the mist which crazed Homer.

These are the vegetables of the deep,
The School-flowers of darkness, swimmers
Of denser darknesses where the sun's rays bend for the last time
And in the sky there burns this shifty jellyfish
That degenerates and flashes and re-forms.

Motes in the eye land is the lid of,
They are plucked out of the green skim milk of the eye.

Fishes are nailed on the wood,
The big Jew stands like Christ, nailing them to the wood,
He scrapes the knife up the grain, the scales fly,
He unnails them, reverses them, nails them again,
Scrapes and the scales fly. He lops off the heads,
Shakes out the guts as if they did not belong in the first place,
And they are flesh for the first time in their lives.

Dear Frau _____:
    Your husband, _____, died in the Camp Hospital on
_____. May I express my sincere sympathy on your
bereavement. _____ was admitted to the Hospital on
_____ with severe symptoms of exhaustion, complaining
of difficulties in breathing and pains in the chest. Despite competent medication and devoted medical attention, it proved
impossible, unfortunately, to keep the patient alive. The de-
ceased voiced no final requests.
                    Camp Commandant, _____

On 5th Street Bunko Certified Embalmer Catholic
Leans in his doorway drawing on a natural Bloom Cigar.
He looks up the street. Even the Puerto Ricans are Jews
And the Chinese Laundry closes on Saturday.

Fifth Sunday after Easter

April's sweet hand in the margins betrayed
Her character in late cursive daffodils;
A gauche mark, but beautiful: a maid.

Nostalgia in the sun . . . When the breeze stills,
The white parchment of the light—the cover
Her declaration came in—touches the breath
Faintly with rakish, innocent perfume.
                              Love her:
For her mistiming, for her longings, for her early death.

In the Ringwood

As I roved out impatiently
Good Friday with my bride
To drink in the rivered Ringwood
The draughty season's pride
A fell dismay held suddenly
Our feet on the green hill-side.

The Yellow Spring on Vinegar Hill,
The smile of Slaney water,
The wind in the withered Ringwood,
Grew dark with ancient slaughter.
My love cried out and I beheld her
Change to Sorrow's daughter.

"Ravenhair, what rending
Set those red lips a-shriek,
And dealt those locks in black lament
Like blows on your white cheek,
That in your looks outlandishly
Both woe and fury speak?"

As sharp a lance as the fatal heron
There on the sunken tree
Will strike in the stones of the river
Was the gaze she bent on me.
O her robe into her right hand
She gathered grievously.

"Many times the civil lover
Climbed that pleasant place,
Many times despairing
Died in his love's face,
His spittle turned to vinegar,
Blood in his embrace.

Love that is every miracle
Is torn apart and rent.
The human turns awry
The poles of the firmament.
The fish's bright side is pierced
And good again is spent.

Though every stem on Vinegar Hill
And stone on the Slaney's bed
And every leaf in the living Ringwood
Builds till it is dead
Yet heart and hand, accomplished,
Destroy until they dread.

Dread, a grey devourer,
Stalks in the shade of love.
The dark that dogs our feet
Eats what is sickened of.
The End that stalks Beginning
Hurries home its drove."

I kissed three times her shivering lips.
I drank their naked chill.
I watched the river shining
Where the heron wiped his bill.
I took my love in my icy arms
In the Spring on Ringwood Hill.

Baggot Street Deserta

Lulled, at silence, the spent attack.
The will to work is laid aside.
The breaking-cry, the strain of the rack,
Yield, are at peace. The window is wide
On a crawling arch of stars, and the night
Reacts faintly to the mathematic
Passion of a cello suite
Plotting the quiet of my attic.
A mile away the river toils
Its buttressed fathoms out to sea;
Tucked in the mountains, many miles
Away from its roaring outcome, a shy
Gasp of waters in the gorse
Is sonnetting origins. Dreamers' heads
Lie mesmerised in Dublin's beds
Flashing with images, Adam's morse.

A cigarette, the moon, a sigh
Of educated boredom, greet
A curlew's lingering threadbare cry
Of common loss. Compassionate,
I add my call of exile, half-
Buried longing, half-serious
Anger and the rueful laugh.
We fly into our risk, the spurious.

Versing, like an exile, makes
A virtuoso of the heart,
Interpreting the old mistakes
And discords in a work of Art
For the One, a private masterpiece
Of doctored recollections. Truth
Concedes, before the dew, its place
In the spray of dried forgettings Youth
Collected when they were a single
Furious undissected bloom.
A voice clarifies when the tingle
Dies out of the nerves of time:
Endure and let the present punish.

Looking backward, all is lost;
The past becomes a fairy bog
Alive with fancies, double crossed
By pad of owl and hoot of dog,
Where shaven, serious-minded men
Appear with lucid theses, after
Which they don the mists again
With trackless, cotton-silly laughter;
Secretly a swollen Burke
Assists a decomposing Hare
To cart a body of good work
With midnight mutterings off somewhere;
The goddess who had light for thighs
Grows feet of dung and takes to bed,
Affronting horror-stricken eyes,
The marsh bird that children dread

I nonetheless inflict, endure,
Tedium, intracordal hurt,
The sting of memory's quick, the drear
Uprooting, burying, prising apart
Of loves a strident adolescent
Spent in doubt and vanity.
All feed a single stream, impassioned
Now with obsessed honesty,
A tugging scruple that can keep
Clear eyes staring down the mile
The thousand fathoms, into sleep.

Fingers cold against the sill
Feel, below the stress of flight,
The slow implosion of my pulse
In a wrist with poet's cramp, a tight
Beat tapping out endless calls
Into the dark, as the alien
Garrison in my own blood
Keeps constant contact with the main
Mystery, not to be understood.
Out where imagination arches
Chilly points of light transact
The business of the border-marches
Of the Real, and I—a fact
That may be countered or may not—
Find their privacy complete.

My quarter-inch of cigarette
Goes flaring down to Baggot Street.

A Country Walk

Sick of the piercing company of women
I swung the gate shut with a furious sigh,
Rammed trembling hands in pockets and drew in
A breath of river air. A rook's wet wing
Cuffed abruptly upward through the drizzle.

On either hand dead trunks in drapes of creeper,
Strangled softly by horse-mushroom, writhed
In vanished passion, broken down like sponge.
I walked their hushed stations, passion dying,
Each slow footfall a drop of peace returning.

I clapped my gloves. Three cattle turned aside
Their fragrant bodies from a corner gate
And down the sucking chaos of a hedge
Churned land to liquid in their dreamy passage.
Briefly through the beaded grass a path
Led to the holy stillness of a well
And there in the smell of water, stone and leaf
I knelt, baring my hand, and scooped and drank,
Shivering, and inch by inch rejoiced:
Ferocity became intensity.

Or so it seemed as with a lighter step
I turned an ivied corner to confront
The littered fields where summer broke and fled.
Below me, right and left, the valley floor
Tilted in a silence full of storms;
A ruined aqueduct in delicate rigor
Clenched cat-backed, rooted to one horizon;
A vast asylum reared its potent calm
Up from the other through the sodden air,
Tall towers ochre where the gutters dripped;
A steeple; the long yielding of a railway turn
Through thorn and willow; a town endured its place . . .

Joining the two slopes, blocking an ancient way
With crumbled barracks, castle and brewery
It took the running river, wrinkling and pouring
Into its blunt embrace. A line of roofs
Fused in veils of rain and steely light
As the dying sun struck it huge glancing blows
A strand of idle smoke mounted until
An idler current combed it slowly west,
A hook of shadow dividing the still sky . . .
Mated, like a fall of rock, with time,
The place endured its burden: as a froth
Locked in a swirl of turbulence, a shape
That forms and fructifies and dies, a wisp
That hugs the bridge, an omphalos of scraps.

I moved, my glove-backs glistening, over flesh-
And forest-fed earth; till, skirting a marshy field
Where melancholy brambles scored the mud
By the gapped glitter of a speckled ford,
I shuddered with a visual sweet excitement.

Those murmuring shallows made a trampling place
Apt for death-combat, as the tales agree:
There, the day that Christ hung dying, twin
Brothers armed in hate on either side;
The day darkened but they moved to meet
With crossed swords under a dread eclipse
And mingled their bowels at the saga's end.
There the first Normans massacred my fathers,
Then stroked their armoured horses' necks, disposed
In ceremony, sable on green sward.
Twice more the reeds grew red, the stones obscured;
When knot-necked Cromwell and his fervent sword
Despatched a convent shrieking to their Lover,
And when in peasant fear a rebel host,
Through long retreat grown half hysterical
—Methodical, ludicrous—piked in groups of three
Cromwell's puritan brood, their harmless neighbours,
Forked them half living to the sharp water
And melted into the martyred countryside,
Root eaters, strange as badgers. Pulses calmed;
The racked heroic nerved itself for peace;

Then came harsh winters, motionless waterbirds,
And generations that let welcome fail.

Road and river parted. Now my path
Lay gleaming through the greasy dusk, uphill
Into the final turn. A concrete cross
Low in the ditch grew to the memory
Of one who answered latest the phantom hag,
Tireless Rebellion, when with mouth awry
She hammered at the door, disrupting harvest.
There he bled to death, his line of sight
Blocked by the corner-stone, and did not see
His town ablaze with joy, the grinning foe
Driven in heavy lorries from the field;
And he lay cold in the Hill Cemetery
When freedom burned his comrades' itchy palms,
Too much for flesh and blood, and—armed in hate—
Brother met brother in a modern light.
They turned the bloody corner, knelt and killed,
Who gather still at Easter round his grave,
Our watchful elders. Deep in his crumbled heart
He takes their soil, and chatting they return
To take their town again, that have exchanged
A trenchcoat playground for a gombeen jungle.

Around the corner, in an open square,
I came upon the sombre monuments
That bear their names: MacDonagh & McBride,
Merchants; Connolly's Commercial Arms . . .
Their windows gave me back my stolid self
In attitudes of staring as I paced
Their otherworldly gloom, reflected light
Playing on lens and raincoat stonily.
I turned away. Down the sloping square
A lamp switched on above the urinal;
Across the silent handball alley, eyes
That never looked on lover measured mine
Over the Christian Brothers' frosted glass
And turned away. Out of the neighboring shades
A car plunged soundlessly and disappeared
Pitching downward steeply to the bridge.
I too descended. Naked sycamores,
Gathered dripping near the quay, stood still

And dropped from their combining arms a single
Word upon my upturned face. I trod
The river underfoot; the parapet
Above the central arch received my hands.

Under a darkening and clearing heaven
The hastening river streamed in a slate sheen,
Its face a-swarm. Across the swollen water
(Delicate myriads vanishing in a breath)
Faint ripples winked; a thousand currents broke,
Kissing, dismembering, in threads of foam
Or poured intact over the stony bed
Glass-green and chill; their shallow, shifting world
Slid on in troubled union, forging together
Surfaces that gave and swallowed light;
And grimly the flood divided where it swept
An endless debris through the failing dusk
Under the thudding span beneath my feet.
Venit Hesperus;
In green and golden light; bringing sweet trade.
The inert stirred. Heart and tongue were loosed:
"The waters hurtle through the flooded night . . ."

Mask of Love

Mask of Love, starting
Aghast out of unreason,
Do you come to us for peace?
Me, flinching from your stare;
Her, whose face you bear!

Remember
How with extreme care
And gentleness we have come,
Aching in heart and throat,
To stand again and again
On peaks of stress, face
To face, wearied with horror,
Yelling in ecstasy
Across the narrow abyss.

(1 2 3)

Remember
That our very bodies lack peace:
In tiny darknesses,
In accustomed hideousness,
The skin angrily flames,
Nerve gropes for muscle
Across the silent abyss.

You have seen our nocturnal
Suicidal dance,
When the moon hung vast, and seemed
To wet our mocking mouths:
She, turning in despair
Round some tiny mote;
I, doubled in laughter,
Clasping my paunch in grief
For the world in a speck of dust;
Between us, the fuming abyss.

Dumb vapours pour
Where the mask of Love appears,
Reddening, and disappears.

CAROLYN KIZER

A Widow in Wintertime

Last night a baby gargled in the throes
Of a fatal spasm. My children are all grown
Past infant strangles; so, reassured, I knew
Some other baby perished in the snow.
But no. The cat was making love again.

(1 2 4)

Later, I went down and let her in.
She hung her tail, flagging from her sins.
Though she'd eaten, I forked out another dinner,
Being myself hungry all ways, and thin
From metaphysic famines she knows nothing of,

The feckless beast! Even so, resemblances
Were on my mind: female and feline, though
She preens herself from satisfaction, and does
Not mind lying even in snow. She is
Lofty and bedraggled, without need to choose.

As an ex-animal, I look fondly on
Her excesses and simplicities and would not return
To them; taking no marks for what I have become,
Merely that my nine lives peal in my ears again
And again, ring in these austerities,

These arbitrary disciplines of mine,
Most of them trivial: like covering
The children on my way to bed, and trying
To live well enough alone, and not to dream
Of grappling in the snow, claws plunged in fur,

Or waken in a caterwaul of dying.

STANLEY KUNITZ

After the Last Dynasty

    Reading in Li Po
    how "the peach blossom follows the water"
    I keep thinking of you
    because you were so much like
    Chairman Mao,

naturally with the sex
transposed
and the figure slighter.
Loving you was a kind
of Chinese guerilla war.
Thanks to your lightfoot genius
no Eighth Route Army
kept its lines more fluid,
traveled with less baggage,
so nibbled the advantage.
Even with your small bad heart
you made a dance of departures.
In the cold spring rains
when last you failed me
I had nothing left to spend
but a red crayon language
on the character of the enemy
to break appointments,
to fight us not
with his strength
but with his weakness,
to kill us
not with his health
but with his sickness.

Pet, spitfire, blue-eyed pony,
here is a new note
I want to pin on your door,
though I am ten years late
and you are nowhere:
Tell me,
are you still mistress of the valley,
what trophies drift down-river,
why did you keep me waiting?

DILYS LAING

Aubade

My bed rocks me gently
in the pale shallows
of 5 A.M.

Lying beside you I wait
for the tree-toad clock-bell
to scream you awake

My ears are full of trees
in which choruses of birds
explode

The great light of morning
shines and shakes
in my eyes

Villanelle

Proud inclination of the flesh,
most upright tendency, salute
in honor of the secret wish.

Slant attitude. When anglers fish
they hold their rods in this acute
proud inclination of the flesh

as purely in the waters thrash
the living fish like silver fruit
in honor of the secret wish.

For who's so risky or so rash
he would forbid this absolute
proud inclination of the flesh?

(1 2 7)

No woman, truly. Let her blush
and hide her thoughts. Herself she'll suit
in honor of the secret wish.

Let scholars all their reasons thresh—
this argument they'll not refute:
proud inclination of the flesh
in honor of the secret wish.

PHILIP   LARKIN

Dry-Point

Endlessly, time-honoured irritant,
A bubble is restively forming at your tip.
Burst it as fast as we can—
It will grow again, until we begin dying.

Silently it inflates, till we're enclosed
And forced to start the struggle to get out:
Bestial, intent, real.
The wet spark comes, the bright blown walls collapse,

But what sad scapes we cannot turn from then:
What ashen hills! what salted, shrunken lakes!
How leaden the ring looks,
Birmingham magic all discredited,

And how remote that bare and sunscrubbed room,
Intensely far, that padlocked cube of light
We neither define nor prove,
Where you, we dream, obtain no right of entry.

Myxomatosis

Caught in the centre of a soundless field
While hot inexplicable hours go by
What trap is this? Where were its teeth concealed?
You seem to ask.
                    I make a sharp reply,
Then clean my stick. I'm glad I can't explain
Just in what jaws you were to suppurate:
You may have thought things would come right again
If you could only keep quite still and wait.

Toads

Why should I let the toad *work*
    Squat on my life?
Can't I use my wit as a pitchfork
    And drive the brute off?

Six days of the week it soils
    With its sickening poison—
Just for paying a few bills!
    That's out of proportion.

Lots of folk live on their wits:
    Lecturers, lispers,
Losels, loblolly-men, louts—
    They don't end as paupers;

Lots of folk live up lanes
    With fires in a bucket,
Eat windfalls and tinned sardines—
    They seem to like it.

Their nippers have got bare feet,
    Their unspeakable wives
Are skinny as whippets—and yet
    No one actually *starves*.

Ah, were I courageous enough
    To shout *Stuff your pension!*
But I know, all too well, that's the stuff
    That dreams are made on:

For something sufficiently toad-like
    Squats in me, too;
Its hunkers are heavy as hard luck,
    And cold as snow,

And will never allow me to blarney
    My way to getting
The fame and the girl and the money
    All at one sitting.

I don't say, one bodies the other
    One's spiritual truth;
But I do say it's hard to lose either,
    When you have both.

Poetry of Departures

Sometimes you hear, fifth-hand,
As epitaph:
He chucked up everything
And just cleared off,
And always the voice will sound
Certain you approve
This audacious, purifying,
Elemental move.

And they are right, I think.
We all hate home
And having to be there:
I detest my room,
Its specially-chosen junk,
The good books, the good bed,
And my life, in perfect order:
So to hear it said

(1 3 0)

He walked out on the whole crowd
Leaves me flushed and stirred,
Like *Then she undid her dress*
Or *Take that you bastard;*
Surely I can, if he did?
And that helps me stay
Sober and industrious.
But I'd go today,

Yes, swagger the nut-strewn roads,
Crouch in the fo'c'sle
Stubbly with goodness, if
It weren't so artificial,
Such a deliberate step backwards
To create an object:
Books; china; a life
Reprehensibly perfect.

Deceptions

"Of course I was drugged, and so heavily I did not
regain my consciousness till the next morning. I was
horrified to discover that I had been ruined, and for
some days I was inconsolable, and cried like a child
to be killed or sent back to my aunt."
—MAYHEW, *London Labour and the London Poor*

Even so distant, I can taste the grief,
Bitter and sharp with stalks, he made you gulp.
The sun's occasional print, the brisk brief
Worry of wheels along the streets outside
Where bridal London bows the other way,
And light, unanswerable and tall and wide,
Forbids the scar to heal, and drives
Shame out of hiding. All the unhurried day
Your mind lay open like a drawer of knives.

(1 3 1)

Slums, years, have buried you. I would not dare
Console you if I could. What can be said,
Except that suffering is exact, but where
Desire takes charge, readings will grow erratic?
For you would hardly care
That you were less deceived, out on that bed,
Than he was, stumbling up the breathless stair
To burst into fulfilment's desolate attic.

IRVING LAYTON

Overheard in a Barbershop

"Nature is blind,
and Man
a shaggy pitiless ape
without Justice,"
the razored
old gentleman said,
his acidulous breath
fogging the barber's
round mirror.
As he talked
I remarked
the naevi, black
and dark purple,
on his crumbling face:
Death's
little victory flags.

Pure Products

To the sea they came—
2000 miles in an old bus
fitted with brittle shelves and makeshift beds
and cluttered with U.S. canned goods
               —to the Sea!
on which they paddle
innertubes   —and the lowhovering Sun—
from which the old woman hides her head
under what looks like
a straw wastebasket.
           "Yep, they cured me alright,
but see, it made my breasts grow like a woman's."
And she: "Something hurts him in his chest,
I think
     maybe it's his heart,"—and her's
I can see beating at the withered throat.

To the Sea some force has driven them—
        away from a lifetime.
And in this windless heat they purpose
to walk the 3 miles of shadeless beach to the store
to ask in Spanish (of which they know
only yes and no) for wholewheat flour
(which is unknown in the region) that she
may bake their bread!
           They are dying
in their gentleness, adorned
with wrinkled apple smiles—nothing
remains for them
but to live a little, invoking
the old powers.

III CRYSTAL NIGHT

From blacked-out streets
   (wide avenues swept by curfew,
   alleyways, veins
   of dark within dark)

from houses whose walls
   had for a long time known
the tense stretch of skin over bone
as their brick or stone listened—

       The scream!
The awaited scream rises,
the shattering
of glass and the cracking
of bone

a polar tumult as when
black ice booms, knives
of ice and glass
splitting and splintering the silence into
innumerable screaming needles of
yes, now it is upon us, the jackboots
are running in spurts of
sudden blood-light through the
broken temples

the veils
are rent in twain
terror has a white sound
every scream
of fear is a white needle freezing the eyes
the floodlights of their trucks throw
jets of white, their shouts
cleave the wholeness of darkness into
sectors of transparent white-clouded pantomime
where all that was awaited
is happening, it is Crystal Night

it is Crystal Night
these spikes which are not
pitched in the range of common hearing
whistle through time

smashing the windows of sleep and dream
smashing the windows of history
a whiteness scattering
in hailstones
each a mirror
for man's eyes.

JOHN LOGAN

Shore Scene

There were bees about. From the start I thought
The day was apt to hurt. There is a high
Hill of sand behind the sea and the kids
Were dropping from the top of it like schools
Of fish over falls, cracking skulls on skulls.
I knew the holiday was hot. I saw
The August sun teeming in the bodies
Logged along the beach and felt the yearning
In the brightly covered parts turning each
To each. For lunch I bit the olive meat:
A yellow jacket stung me on the tongue.
I knelt to spoon and suck the healing sea . . .
A little girl was digging up canals
With her toes, her arm hanging in a cast
As white as the belly of a dead fish
Whose dead eye looked at her with me, as she
Opened her grotesque system to the see . . .
I walked away; now quietly I heard
A child moaning from a low mound of sand,

Abandoned by his friend. The child was tricked,
Trapped upon his knees in a shallow pit.
(The older ones will say you can get out.)
I dug him up. His legs would not unbend.
I lifted him and held him in my arms
As he wept. Oh I was gnarled as a witch
Or warlock by his naked weight, was slowed
In the sand to a thief's gait. When his strength
Flowed, he ran, and I rested by the sea . . .
A girl was there. I saw her drop her hair,
Let it fall from the doffed cap to her breasts
Tanned and swollen over wine red woolen.
A boy, his body blackened by the sun,
Rose out of the sand stripping down his limbs
With graceful hands. He took his gear and walked
Toward the girl in the brown hair and wine
And then past me; he brushed her with the soft
Brilliant monster he lugged into the sea . . .
By this tide I raised a small cairn of stone
Light and smooth and clean, and cast the shadow
Of a stick in a perfect line along
The sand. My own shadow followed then, until
I felt the cold swirling at the groin.

FROM *A Trip to Four or Five Towns*

In New York I got drunk, to tell the truth,
and almost got locked up when a beat
friend with me took a leak in a telephone booth.
(E. E. Cummings on the Paris lawn.
"Reprieve pisseur Américain!")
At two o'clock he got knocked out
horning in with the girl in the room over him.
Her boy friend was still sober,
and too thin. I saw the blood of a poet
flow on the sidewalk. Oh, if I mock,
it is without heart. I thought
of the torn limbs of Orpheus
scattered in the grass on the hills of Thrace.
Do poets have to have such trouble with the female race?

(*1 3 6*)

I do not know. But if they bleed
I lose heart also.
When he reads, ah, when he reads, small but deep voiced,
he reads well: now weeps, now is cynical,
his large, horned eyes very black and tearful.

And when we visited a poet father
we rode to Jersey on a motor scooter.
My tie and tweeds looped in the winds.
I choked in the wake
Of the Holland Pipe, and cops,
under glass like carps, eyed us.
That old father was so mellow and generous—
easy to pain,
white, open and at peace, and of good taste,
like his Rutherford house.
And he read, very loud and regal,
sixteen new poems based on paintings by Breughel!

ROBERT LOWELL

FROM *The Quaker Graveyard in Nantucket*

FOR WARREN WINSLOW, DEAD AT SEA

Let man have dominion over the fishes of the sea and the
fowls of the air and the beasts and the whole earth, and
every creeping creature that moveth upon the earth.

I

A brackish reach of shoal off Madaket,—
The sea was still breaking violently and night
Had steamed into our North Atlantic Fleet,
When the drowned sailor clutched the drag-net. Light
flashed from his matted head and marble feet,

He grappled at the net
With the coiled, hurdling muscles of his thighs:
The corpse was bloodless, a botch of reds and whites,
Its open, staring eyes
Were lustreless dead-lights
Or cabin-windows on a stranded hulk
Heavy with sand. We weight the body, close
Its eyes and heave it seaward whence it came,
Where the heel-headed dogfish barks its nose
On Ahab's void and forehead; and the name
Is blocked in yellow chalk.
Sailors, who pitch this portent at the sea
Where dreadnaughts shall confess
Its hell-bent deity,
When you are powerless
To sand-bag this Atlantic bulwark, faced
By the earth-shaker, green, unwearied, chaste
In his steel scales: ask for no Orphean lute
To pluck life back. The guns of the steeled fleet
Recoil and then repeat
The hoarse salute.

II

Whenever winds are moving and their breath
Heaves at the roped-in bulwarks of this pier,
The terns and sea-gulls tremble at your death
In these home waters. Sailor, can you hear
The Pequod's sea wings, beating landward, fall
Headlong and break on our Atlantic wall
Off 'Sconset, where the yawing S-boats splash
The bellbuoy, with ballooning spinnakers,
As the entangled, screeching mainsheet clears
The blocks: off Madaket, where lubbers lash
The heavy surf and throw their long lead squids
For blue-fish? Sea-gulls blink their heavy lids
Seaward. The winds' wings beat upon the stones,
Cousin, and scream for you and the claws rush
At the sea's throat and wring it in the slush
Of this old Quaker graveyard where the bones
Cry out in the long night for the hurt beast
Bobbing by Ahab's whaleboats in the East.

A Mad Negro Soldier Confined at Munich

"We're all Americans, except the Doc,
a Kraut DP, who kneels and bathes my eye.
The boys who floored me, two black maniacs, try
to pat my hands. Rounds, rounds! Why punch the clock?

In Munich the zoo's rubble fumes with cats;
hoydens with air-guns prowl the Koenigsplatz,
and pink the pigeons on the mustard spire.
Who but my girl-friend set the town on fire?

Cat-houses talk cold turkey to my guards;
I found my *Fräulein* stitching outing shirts
in the black forest of the colored wards—
lieutenants squawked like chickens in her skirts.

Her German language made my arteries harden—
I've no annuity from the pay we blew.
I chartered an aluminum canoe,
I had her six times in the English Garden.

Oh mama, mama, like a trolley-pole
sparking at contact, her electric shock—
the power-house! . . . The doctor calls our roll—
no knives, no forks. We file before the clock,

and fancy minnows, slaves of habit, shoot
like starlight through their air-conditioned bowl.
It's time for feeding. Each subnormal boot-
black heart is pulsing to its ant-egg dole."

Words for Hart Crane

"When the Pulitzers showered on some dope
or screw who flushed our dry mouths out with soap,
few people would consider why I took
to stalking sailors, and scattered Uncle Sam's
phoney gold-plated laurels to the birds.

(1 3 9)

Because I knew my Whitman like a book,
stranger in America, tell my country: I,
Catullus redivivus, once the rage
of the Village and Paris, used to play my role
of homosexual, wolfing the stray lambs
who hungered by the Place de la Concorde.
My profit was a pocket with a hole.
Who asks for me, the Shelley of my age,
must lay his heart out for my bed and board."

Skunk Hour

FOR ELIZABETH BISHOP

Nautilus Island's hermit
heiress still lives through winter in her Spartan cottage;
her sheep still graze above the sea.
Her son's a bishop. Her farmer
is first selectman in our village;
she's in her dotage.

Thirsting for
the hierarchic privacy
of Queen Victoria's century,
she buys up all
the eyesores facing her shore,
and lets them fall.

The season's ill—
we've lost our summer millionaire,
who seemed to leap from an L. L. Bean
catalogue. His nine-knot yawl
was auctioned off to lobstermen.
A red fox stain covers Blue Hill.

And now our fairy
decorator brightens his shop for fall;
his fishnet's filled with orange cork,
orange, his cobbler's bench and awl;
there is no money in his work,
he'd rather marry.

One dark night,
my Tudor Ford climbed the hill's skull;
I watched for love-cars. Lights turned down,
they lay together, hull to hull,
where the graveyard shelves on the town. . . .
My mind's not right.

A car radio bleats,
"Love, O careless Love. . . ." I hear
my ill-spirit sob in each blood cell,
as if my hand were at its throat. . . .
I myself am hell;
nobody's here—

only skunks, that search
in the moonlight for a bite to eat.
They march on their soles up Main Street:
white stripes, moonstruck eyes' red fire
under the chalk-dry and spar spire
of the Trinitarian Church.

I stand on top
of our back steps and breathe the rich air—
a mother skunk with her column of kittens swills the garbage
        pail.
She jabs her wedge-head in a cup
of sour cream, drops her ostrich tail,
and will not scare.

To Delmore Schwartz

Cambridge 1946

We couldn't even keep the furnace lit!
Even when we had disconnected it,
the antiquated
refrigerator gurgled mustard gas
through your mustard-yellow house,
and spoiled our long maneuvered visit
from T. S. Eliot's brother, Henry Ware. . . .

Your stuffed duck craned toward Harvard from my trunk:
its bill was a black whistle, and its brow
was high and thinner than a baby's thumb;
its webs were tough as toenails on its bough.
It was your first kill; you had rushed it home,
pickled in a tin wastebasket of rum—
it looked through us, as if it'd died dead drunk.
You must have propped its eyelids with a nail,
and yet it lived with us and met our stare,
Rabelaisian, lubricious, drugged. And there,
perched on my trunk and typing-table,
it cooled our universal
Angst a moment, Delmore. We drank and eyed
the chicken-hearted shadows of the world.
Underseas fellows, nobly mad,
we talked away our friends. "Let Joyce and Freud,
the Masters of Joy,
be our guests here," you said. The room was filled
with cigarette smoke circling the paranoid,
inert gaze of Coleridge, back
from Malta—his eyes lost in flesh, lips baked and black.
Your tiger kitten, *Oranges,*
cartwheeled for joy in a ball of snarls.
You said:
"*We poets in our youth begin in sadness;
thereof in the end come despondency and madness;*
Stalin has had two cerebral hemorrhages!"
The Charles
River was turning silver. In the ebb-
light of morning, we stuck
the duck
-'s web-
foot, like a candle, in a quart of gin we'd killed.

For the Union Dead

"Relinquunt omnia servare rem publicam."

The old South Boston Aquarium stands
in a Sahara of snow now. Its broken windows are boarded.
The bronze weathervane cod has lost half its scales.
The airy tanks are dry.

Once my nose crawled like a snail on the glass;
my hand tingled
to burst the bubbles
drifting from the noses of the cowed, compliant fish.

My hand draws back. I often sigh still
for the dark downward and vegetating kingdom
of the fish and reptile. One morning last March,
I pressed against the new barbed and galvanized

fence on the Boston Common. Behind their cage,
yellow dinosaur steamshovels were grunting
as they cropped up tons of mush and grass
to gouge their underworld garage.

Parking-spaces luxuriate like civic
sandpiles in the heart of Boston.
A girdle of orange, Puritan-pumpkin colored girders
braces the tingling Statehouse,

shaking over the excavations, as it faces Colonel Shaw
and his bell-cheeked Negro infantry
on St. Gaudens' shaking Civil War relief,
propped by a plank splint against the garage's earthquake.

Two months after marching through Boston,
half the regiment was dead;
at the dedication,
William James could almost hear the bronze Negroes breathe.

Their monument sticks like a fishbone
in the City's throat.
Its Colonel is as lean
as a compass-needle.

He has an angry wrenlike vigilance,
a greyhound's gentle tautness;
he seems to wince at pleasure,
and suffocate for privacy.

(143)

He is out of bounds now. He rejoices in man's lovely,
peculiar power to choose life and die—
when he leads his black soldiers to death,
he cannot bend his back.

On a thousand small town New England greens,
the old white churches hold their air
of sparse, sincere rebellion; frayed flags
quilt the graveyards of the Grand Army of the Republic.

The stone statues of the abstract Union Soldier
grow slimmer and younger each year—
wasp-waisted, they doze over muskets
and muse through their sideburns . . .

Shaw's father wanted no monument
except the ditch,
where his son's body was thrown
and lost with his "niggers."

The ditch is nearer.
There are no statues for the last war here;
on Boylston Street, a commercial photograph
shows Hiroshima boiling

over a Mosler Safe, the "Rock of Ages"
that survived the blast. Space is nearer.
When I crouch to my television set,
the drained faces of Negro school-children rise like balloons.

Colonel Shaw
is riding on his bubble,
he waits
for the blessèd break.

The Aquarium is gone. Everywhere,
giant finned cars nose forward like fish;
a savage servility
slides by on grease.

Child's Song

My cheap toy lamp
gives little light
all night, all night,
when my muscles cramp.

Sometimes I touch your hand
across my cot,
and our fingers knot,
but there's no hand

to take me home—
no Caribbean
island, where even
the shark is at home.

It must be heaven.
There on that island
the white sand shines
like a birchwood fire.

Help, saw me in two,
put me on the shelf!
Sometimes the little muddler
can't stand itself!

The Lesson

No longer to lie reading "Tess of the d'Urbervilles,"
while the high, mysterious squirrels
rain small green branches on our sleep!

All that landscape, one likes to think it died
or slept with us, that we ourselves died
or slept then in the age and second of our habitation.

The green leaf cushions the same dry footprint,
or the child's boat luffs in the same dry chop,
and we are where we were. We were!

(1 4 5)

Perhaps the trees stopped growing in summer amnesia;
their day that gave them veins is rooted down—
and the nights? They are for sleeping now as then.

Ah the light lights the window of my young night,
and you never turn off the light,
while the books lie in the library, and go on reading.

The barberry fruit sticks on the small hedge,
cold slices the same crease in the finger,
the same thorn hurts. The leaf repeats the lesson.

GEORGE   MACBETH

Ash

So it was true. Elastic air could fill
        In a trice with particles
    And clapped earth give no warning. Ill
        With rage, they swallowed pills,
Floundered to hide-outs. Over the hogback Southern hills

    A giant sifter shook black sugar. Bleeps
        On the tele-screen spelled SLEEP
    IT THROUGH. Eyes glued on sky-fed slag-heaps
        Peppering soot, watched sheep
Whose wool stank acrid stick at stiles no legs could leap.

    The crushed air gently settled. In a slow
        Powdering like a crow's
    Wing mouldering, a thin tar snow
        Assembled, staining toes
Of barefoot children dug in sand it cast no shadows

In but mingled with. What fitter night
        For prophesying flights
        Of rooks? In entrails needles might
        Probe omens. Grilled in tights,
A Creole whore screamed giving birth. Her brat's paired whites

        Shone like burnt coals. A negro steeplejack
        Nine floors up welding cracks
        In scaffolding shrivelled on a rack
        Of poisoned iron. Packs
Of wolves burned. Chessboard queens in stained teak spat like
        sacks

        Of roasted chestnuts on a grated fire
        Of sulphur. A Church choir's
        Top alto charred. His Chrysler tyre
        Made licorice. The spire's
Incinerating copper boiled a bat. *Esquires*

        Where clutching fingers curled, shrank into what
        Crumbled like bad flour, blots
        Of putrefying matter, hot
        As frying kidneys. Shots
Of iced Scotch would have cooled one soldier's nerve-ends.
        Dots

        And dashes flustered angry dials. Done
        Steaks grilled. Not everyone's
        Plop-footed warden, won
        From melting wax, brought guns
To fortify stuffed cellars. When one came, few suns,

        Rotting the bricked fumes, twisted through taut sashes
        To explore a livid gash
        Of wounded air where crackling lashes
        Writhed. More times that rash
Of acid yellow faltered. What was left was ash.

(*1 4 7*)

Mother Superior

Sisters, it will be necessary
To prepare a cool retreat. See to
It that several basins are filled
Nightly with fresh water and placed there.
Take care that food for a long stay be

Provided in sealed jars. I know of
No way to protect an outer room
From the light but some must be tried. Let
The walls be made thick to keep out the
Heat. Before the Annunciation

Our Lord exacts no other service.
It may seem prudent to wear a wool
Robe at all times and to bow down when
The Word comes. Remember the parable
Of the Virgins and pray for all the

Unpremeditating. "The brides of
Our Lord in their burrows" may not be
A flattering title but the known
Future lies in the wombs of prepared
Rabbits. To bear a pure strain with no

Care for the world's corruption requires
Courage, sisters. Creating a safe
Place for the incarnation of what
One can scarcely imagine without
Madness might seem a demeaning task.

In the Order of Resurrection
Of which you are acolytes there is
No more noble service. Remember
The Code. Your duty is not to the
Sick but to the unborn. Perform it.

"The Spider's Nest

Was clenched on a fly's carcase like a golden
Fist which exploded into an abacus
Of excited beads at the prick of my quill"

Is one verse. "This morning I arranged about
A hundred things with legs on invisible
Wires to dance attendance" is another. To

Be crippled and have such tensed will subdued by
A feather pleases. On a wheeled bed or an
Orbed web life rakes old sores over with my (or

Some other) tough hand. The feather of death in
One's bowels tickles the triumph out of such
Teasing of puissance. Day after day to lie

Here watching the sun skate in the sky, wanting
Death but unable to move except enough
To kill wasps with a book or annoy spiders,

Is something. After all, success in drowning
Ants in vermouth requires only time and I
Collect it like dust. Snakes come. Visitors with

French sonnets. Minestrone for supper. Floods
In May. If Stock insists on a third verse I
Suggest "a few hesitated between the

Abrupt brink of air and the known centre of
A gauze mesh where their inherited fly lay
Spread out to be eaten" but I'm not keen on

A fourth verse. To leave great themes unfinished is
Perhaps the most satisfying exercise
Of power. Describing their look of being

The armour of a god left hanging over-
night in a skein of frost can be decently
Left to Vernon. Sleep comes. And with it my snails.

Florence, 1885, Eugene Lee-Hamilton.

(*1 4 9*)

Innocence

What answer could she give
To the leopard in the dark?
To the clawed flower? to the dappled, twitching grass?
Only her own desire in which to live
Where anything might pass
And leave, such was its radiance, no mark.

The words that wounded her
Became part of her speech.
The face she feared looked through her gentle eyes;
And when she moved, midnight began to stir.
A world of muffled cries
Became the only world that she could reach.

She thought that radiance dead—
She who could not be seen,
Invisible in its brightness, now she was
Part of what it shone on. She drooped her head
And, soft as a leopard's paws,
Moused in the dark for what she once had been.

November Night, Edinburgh

The night tinkles like ice in glasses.
Leaves are glued to the pavement with frost.
The brown air fumes at the shop windows,
Tries the doors, and sidles past.

I gulp down winter raw. The heady
Darkness swirls with tenements.
In a brown fuzz of cottonwool
Lamps fade up crags, die into pits.

Frost in my lungs is harsh as leaves
Scraped up on paths.—I look up, there,
A high roof sails, at the mast-head
Fluttering a gray and ragged star.

The world's a bear shrugged in his den.
It's snug and close in the snoring night.
And outside like chrysanthemums
The fog unfolds its bitter scent.

Edinburgh Spring

I walk my paint-box suburb. The clear air
Is flecked with green and ultramarine and rose.
The wind hangs nursery rhymes on branches;
The sun leans ladders against the apple trees.

And all my defence against the advancing summer
Is to trim hedges, gush the gutters sweet,
Tie the doomed rose against the wall
And watch myself being young and innocent.

Trams from my innocence thunder by like suns
Through my familiar city to where I know
Slatternly tenements wait till night
To make a Middle Ages in the sky.

A buzzing gas-lamp there must be my rose
Eating itself away in the ruined air
Where a damp bannister snakes up and
Time coughs his lungs out behind a battered door.

There craggy windows blink, mad buildings toss
Dishevelled roofs, and dangerous shadows lean,
Heavy with centuries, against the walls;
And Spring walks by ashamed, her eyes cast down.

(1 5 1)

She's not looked at. O merry midnight when
Squalid Persepolis shrugs its rotting stone
Round its old bones and hears the crowds
Weeping and cheering and crying, "Tamburlaine."

HUGH MACDIARMID

The Spanish War

Ah, Spain, already your tragic landscapes
And the agony of your War to my mind appear
As tears may come into the eyes of a woman very slowly,
So slowly as to leave them CLEAR!

Spain! The International Brigade! At the moment it seems
As though the pressure of a loving hand had gone,
(Till the next proletarian upsurge!)
The touch under which my close-pressed fingers seemed to
thrill,
And the skin to divide up into little zones
Of heat and cold whose position continually changed,
So that the whole of my hand, held in that clasp,
Was in a state of internal movement.
My eyes that were full of pride,
My hands that were full of love,
Are empty again . . . for a while.
                    For a little while!

British Leftish Poetry, 1930–40

Auden, MacNeice, Day Lewis, I have read them all,
Hoping against hope to hear the authentic call.
"A tragical disappointment. There was I
Hoping to hear old Aeschylus, when the Herald

Called out, 'Theognis, bring your chorus forward.'
Imagine what my feelings must have been!
But then Dexitheus pleased me coming forward
And singing his Bœotian melody:
But next came Chaeris with his music truly
That turned me sick and killed me very nearly.
And never in my lifetime, man nor boy,
Was I so vexed as at the present moment;
To see the Pynx, at this time of the morning,
Quite empty, when the Assembly should be full"*
And know the explanation I must pass is this
—You cannot light a match on a crumbling wall.

Reflections in a Slum

A lot of the old folk here—all that's left
Of them after a lifetime's infernal thrall
Remind me of a Bolshie the "whites" buried alive
Up to his nose, just able to breathe, that's all.

Watch them. You'll see what I mean. When found
His eyes had lost their former gay twinkle.
Ants had eaten *that* away; but there was still
Some life in him . . . his forehead *would* wrinkle!
And I remember Gide telling
Of Valéry and himself:
"It was a long time ago. We were young.
We had mingled with idlers
Who formed a circle
Round a troupe of wretched mountebanks.
It was on a raised strip of pavement
In the boulevard Saint Germain,
In front of the Statue of Broca.
They were admiring a poor woman,
Thin and gaunt, in pink tights, despite the cold.
Her team-mate had tied her, trussed her up,
Skilfully from head to foot,

*Aristophanes, *The Acharnians.*

With a rope that went round her
I don't know how many times,
And from which, by a sort of wriggling,
She was to manage to free herself.
Sorry image of the fate of the masses!
But no one thought of the symbol.
The audience merely contemplated
In stupid bliss the patient's efforts.
She twisted, she writhed, slowly freed one arm,
Then the other, and when at last
The final cord fell from her
Valéry took me by the arm:
'Let's go now! She has ceased suffering!' "

Oh, if only ceasing to suffer
They were able to become men.
Alas! how many owe their dignity,
Their claim on our sympathy,
Merely to their misfortune.
Likewise, so long as a plant has not blossomed
One can hope that its flowering will be beautiful.
What a mirage surrounds what has not yet blossomed!
What a disappointment when one can no longer
Blame the abjection on the deficiency!
It is good that the voice of the indigent,
Too long stifled, should manage
To make itself heard.
But I cannot consent to listen
To nothing but that voice.
Man does not cease to interest me
When he ceases to be miserable.
Quite the contrary!
That it is important to aid him
In the beginning goes without saying,
Like a plant it is essential
To water at first,
But this is in order to get it to flower
And I *am concerned with the blossom.*

Old Wife in High Spirits

In an Edinburgh Pub

An auld wumman cam' in, a mere rickle o' banes, in a faded
        black dress
And a bonnet wi' beads o' jet rattlin' on it;
A puir-lookin' cratur, you'd think she could haurdly ha'e had less
Life left in her and still lived, but dagonit!

He gied her a stiff whisky—she was nervous as a troot
And could haurdly haud the tumbler, puir cratur;
Syne he gied her anither, joked wi' her, and anither, and syne
Wild as the whisky up cam' her nature.

The rod that struck water frae the rock in the desert
Was naething to the life that sprang oot o' her;
The dowie auld soul was twinklin' and fizzin' wi' fire;
You never saw ocht sae souple and kir.

Like a sackful o' monkeys she was, and her lauchin'
Loupit up whiles to incredible heights;
Wi' ane owre the eight her temper changed and her tongue
Flew juist as the forkt lichtnin' skites.

The heich skeich auld cat was fair in her element;
Wanton as a whirlwind, and shairly better that way
Than a' crippen thegither wi' laneliness and cauld
Like a foretaste o' the graveyaird clay.

Some folk nae doot'll condemn gie'in' a guid spree
To the puir dune body and raither she endit her days
Like some auld tashed copy o' the Bible yin sees
On a street book-barrow's tipenny trays.

A' I ken is weel-fed and weel-put-on though they be
Ninety per cent o' respectable folk never hae
As muckle life in their creeshy carcases frae beginnin' to end
As kythed in that wild auld carline that day!

Eurynome

Come all old maids that are squeamish
And afraid to make mistakes,
Don't clutter your lives up with boyfriends:
The nicest girls marry snakes.

If you don't mind slime on your pillow
And caresses as gliding as ice
—Cold skin, warm heart, remember,
And besides, they keep down the mice—

If you're really serious-minded,
It's the best advice you can take:
No rumpling, no sweating, no nonsense,
Oh who would not sleep with a snake?

Fog-Horn

Surely that moan is not the thing
That men thought they were making, when they
Put it there, for their own necessities.
That throat does not call to anything human
But to something men had forgotten,
That stirs under fog. Who wounded that beast
Incurably, or from whose pasture
Was it lost, full grown, and time closed round it
With no way back? Who tethered its tongue
So that its voice could never come

To speak out in the light of clear day,
But only when the shifting blindness
Descends and is acknowledged among us,
As though from under a floor it is heard,
Or as though from behind a wall, always
Nearer than we had remembered? If it
Was we that gave tongue to this cry
What does it bespeak in us, repeating
And repeating, insisting on something
That we never meant? We only put it there
To give warning of something we dare not
Ignore, lest we should come upon it
Too suddenly, recognize it too late,
As our cries were swallowed up and all hands lost.

Bucolic

Having enough plowshares,
The best will in the world, and fat pastures,
They beat the rest of their swords into shears.

The rewards of peace
They reap! With each haired, maned, shag beast,
As each tamed field, fattened for its fleece.

If, as of old,
But with stuffed bellies, the shorn wolves seek the fold,
It is only in winter, from the cold:

Whole days, when the snow is deep,
They lie, pink and harmless, among the sheep,
Nodding, whether in agreement or sleep.

Tanker

She was built for the hard voyage,
tropical havoc. Rats chafe
her comet-coloured hulk, her shadow
is moored, her bells mute
as at matins. She was made
to forge through dry winds
hammering horizons and sperm
of the iron Atlantic's drowned.
And she is chained
inert in granite, enmeshed
by the engineers. Her spars
sag. Her dining-room is deserted.
Only the whores
sway by wherever at high noon
Lascars tiptoe, spit,
and await orders.

The Dress

Her blue dress lightly
Is all my care.
Nothing I am
When not beside her.
Not every day,
Not any hour she passes,
Not always when she passes
Am I enough eager.

Not enough the streetcorner,
Nor the quiet room,
To take her body in.
Not enough the colour

Of patience, of murder
To draw her down
From the balcony she leans upon,
Highcrowned

And in the nighttime turned
Pale into amber over arch,
Inviolate sun.
Not enough the table
Under the awning, nor the elbow
Moving for me to see her,
For she must come
Unseen, without wanting:

Then I shall lightly
With all my care
Have my hand under
Her blue dress when she is there.

The Ancestors

When they come, we begin to go;
it's the ancestors,
they walk into the warm rooms,

eye our women and food, hear out
the good words. Then for words
and rooms we no more exist,

once the ancestors have come,
than a little dust on a vase,
than the breath wasted.

How do they come? They make no
parade of moans and winds;
they borrow no fears, none.

I am persuaded they have come
by the strength of shoes,
by the one shirt extra,

but if most by the bloody love
my shoes and my shirt need
to be seen that way,

I tell myself this is a thing
they'd far better not know,
who have lost the knack,

and only accuse, by the malice
they march us out with, from one
to the next lost place.

JOHN   MONTAGUE

Murphy in Manchester

He wakes to a confused dream of boats, gulls,
And all his new present floats
Suddenly up to him on rocking rails.
Through that long first day
He trudges streets, tracks friends,
Stares open-mouthed at monuments
To manufacturers, sabred generals.
Passing a vegetable stall
With exposed fruits, he halts
To contemplate a knobbly potato
With excitement akin to love.
At lunchtime, in a cafeteria,
He finds his feet and hands
Enlarge, become like foreign lands.
A great city is darkness, noise
Through which bright girls move
Like burnished other children's toys.
Soon the whistling factory
Will lock him in:
Half-stirred memories and regrets
Drowning in that iron din.

Poisoned Lands

In the Irish countryside one often sees crudely painted
signs: THESE LANDS ARE POISONED. This indicates
that meat injected with poison has been laid down to
destroy predatory animals: the practice is not highly
regarded.

"Four good dogs dead in one night
And a rooster, scaly legs in the air,
Beak in the dust, a terrible sight!"
Behind high weathered walls, his share
Of local lands, the owner skulks
Or leaves in dismal guttering gaps
A trail of broken branches, roots,
Bruised by his mournful rubber boots.

Neighbors sight him as a high hat
Dancing down hedges, a skeletal shape
Night-haloed with whistling bats,
Or silhouetted against cloudy skies,
Coat turned briskly to the nape,
Sou'westered in harsh surmise.

"Children dawdling home from Mass
Chased a bouncing ball and found,
Where he had stood, scorched tufts of grass
Blighted leaves"—and here the sound
Of rodent Gossip sank—"worse by far,
Dark radiance as though a star
Had disintegrated, a clinging stench
Gutting the substances of earth and air."

At night, like baleful shadowed eyes,
His windows show the way to cars
Igniting the dark like fireflies.
Gusts of song and broken glass
Prelude wild triumphal feasts
Climaxed by sacrifice of beasts.

*

Privileged, I met him on an evening walk,
Inveigled him into casual weather talk.
"I don't like country people" he said, with a grin.
The winter sunlight halved his mottled chin
And behind, a white notice seemed to swing and say:
"If you too licked grass, you'd be dead to-day."

The First Invasion of Ireland

FOR MICHAEL WALSH

According to Leabhar Gabhàla's *The Book of Conquests,* the first invasion of Ireland was by relatives of Noah, just before the Flood. Refused entry into the Ark, they consulted an idol which told them to flee to Ireland. There were three men and fifty-one women in the party and their behaviour has so little common with subsequent tradition in Ireland that one must take the story to be mythological.

Fleeing from threatened flood, they sailed,
Seeking the fair island, without serpent or claw;
From the deck of their hasty windjammer watched
The soft edge of Ireland nearward draw.

A sweet confluence of waters, a trinity of rivers,
Was their first resting place:
They unloaded the women and the sensual idol,
Guiding image of their disgrace.

Division of damsels they did there,
The slender, the tender, the dimpled, the round,
It was the first just bargain in Ireland,
There was enough to go round.

Lightly they lay and pleasured
In the green grass of that guileless place:
Ladhra was the first to die;
He perished of an embrace.

Bith was buried in a stone heap,
Riot of mind, all passion spent.
Fintan fled from the ferocious women
Before he, too, by love was rent.

Great primitive princes of our line
They were the first, with stately freedom,
To sleep with women in Ireland:
Soft the eternal bed they lie upon.

On a lonely headland the women assembled,
Chill as worshippers in a nave,
And watched the eastern waters gather
Into a great virile flooding wave.

The Trout

FOR BARRIE COOKE

Flat on the bank I parted
Rushes to ease my hands
In the water without a ripple
And tilt them slowly downstream
To where he lay, light as a leaf,
In his fluid sensual dream.

Bodiless lord of creation
I hung briefly above him
Savouring my own absence
Senses expanding in the slow
Motion, the photographic calm
That comes before action.

As the curve of my hands
Swung under his body
He surged, with visible pleasure.
I was so preternaturally close
I could count every stipple
But still cast no shadow, until

(163)

The two palms crossed in a cage
Under the lightly pulsing gills.
Then (entering my own enlarged
Shape, which rode on the water)
I gripped. To this day I can
Taste his terror on my hands.

E D W I N   M U I R

The Horses

Barely a twelvemonth after
The seven days war that put the world to sleep,
Late in the evening the strange horses came.
By then we had made our covenant with silence,
But in the first few days it was so still
We listened to our breathing and were afraid.
On the second day
The radios failed; we turned the knobs; no answer.
On the third day a warship passed us, heading north,
Dead bodies piled on the deck. On the sixth day
A plane plunged over us into the sea. Thereafter
Nothing. The radios dumb;
And still they stand in corners of our kitchens,
And stand, perhaps, turned on, in a million rooms
All over the world. But now if they should speak,
If on a sudden they should speak again,
If on the stroke of noon a voice should speak,
We would not listen, we would not let it bring
That old bad world that swallowed its children quick
At one great gulp. We would not have it again.
Sometimes we think of the nations lying asleep,
Curled blindly in impenetrable sorrow,
And then the thought confounds us with its strangeness.

The tractors lie about our fields; at evening
They look like dank sea-monsters couched and waiting.
We leave them where they are and let them rust:
'They'll moulder away and be like other loam.'
We make our oxen drag our rusty ploughs,
Long laid aside. We have gone back
Far past our fathers' land.
                              And then, that evening
Late in the summer the strange horses came.
We heard a distant tapping on the road,
A deepening drumming; it stopped, went on again
And at the corner changed to hollow thunder.
We saw the heads
Like a wild wave charging and were afraid.
We had sold our horses in our fathers' time
To buy new tractors. Now they were strange to us
As fabulous steeds set on an ancient shield
Or illustrations in a book of knights.
We did not dare go near them. Yet they waited,
Stubborn and shy, as if they had been sent
By an old command to find our whereabouts
And that long-lost archaic companionship.
In the first moment we had never a thought
That they were creatures to be owned and used.
Among them were some half-a-dozen colts
Dropped in some wilderness of the broken world,
Yet new as if they had come from their own Eden.
Since then they have pulled our ploughs and borne our loads,
But that free servitude still can pierce our hearts.
Our life is changed; their coming our beginning.

Sailing to an Island

The boom above my knees lifts, and the boat
Drops, and the surge departs, departs, my cheek
Kissed and rejected, kissed, as the gaff sways
A tangent, cuts the infinite sky to red
Maps, and the mast draws eight and eight across
Measureless blue, the boatmen sing or sleep.

We point all day for our chosen island,
Clare, with its crags purpled by legend:
There under castles the hot O'Malleys,
Daughters of Granuaile, the pirate queen
Who boarded a Turk with a blunderbuss,
Comb red hair and assemble cattle.
Across the shelved Atlantic groundswell
Plumbed by the sun's kingfisher rod,
We sail to locate in sea, earth and stone
The myth of a shrewd and brutal swordswoman
Who piously endowed an abbey.
Seven hours we try against wind and tide,
Tack and return, making no headway.
The north wind sticks like a gag in our teeth.

Encased in a mirage, steam on the water,
Loosely we coast where hideous rocks jag,
An acropolis of cormorants, an extinct
Volcano where spiders spin, a purgatory
Guarded by hags and bristled with breakers.

The breeze as we plunge slowly stiffens:
There are hills of sea between us and land,
Between our hopes and the island harbour.
A child vomits. The boat veers and bucks
There is no refuge on the gannet's cliff.
We are far, far out: the hull is rotten,
The spars are splitting, the rigging is frayed,
And our helmsman laughs uncautiously.

(1 6 6)

What of those who must earn their living
On the ribald face of a mad mistress?
We in holiday fashion know
This is the boat that belched its crew
Dead on the shingle in the Cleggan disaster.

Now she dips, and the sail hits the water.
She hoves to a squall; is struck; and shudders.
Someone is shouting. The boom, weak as scissors,
Has snapped. The boatman is praying.
Orders thunder and canvas cannonades.
She smothers in spray. We still have a mast;
The oar makes a boom. I am told to cut
Cords out of fishing-lines, fasten the jib.
Ropes lash my cheeks. Ease! Ease at last:
She swings to leeward, we can safely run.
Washed over rails our Clare Island dreams,
With storm behind us we straddle the wakeful
Waters that draw us headfast to Inishbofin.

The bows rock as she overtakes the surge.
We neither sleep nor sing nor talk,
But look to the land where the men are mowing.
What will the islanders think of our folly?
The whispering spontaneous reception committee
Nods and smokes by the calm jetty.
Am I jealous of these courteous fishermen
Who hand us ashore, for knowing the sea
Intimately, for respecting the storm
That took nine of their men on one bad night
And five from Rossadillisk in this very boat?
Their harbour is sheltered. They are slow to tell
The story again. There is local pride
In their home-built ships.
We are advised to return next day by the mail.

But tonight we stay, drinking with people
Happy in the monotony of boats,
Bringing the catch to the Cleggan market,
Cultivating fields, or retiring from America
With enough to soak till morning or old age.

The bench below my knees lifts, and the floor
Drops, and the words depart, depart, with faces
Blurred by the smoke. An old man grips my arm,
His shot eyes twitch, quietly dissatisfied.
He has lost his watch, an American gold
From Boston gas-works. He treats the company
To the secretive surge, the sea of his sadness.
I slip outside, fall among stones and nettles,
Crackling dry twigs on an elder tree
While an accordion drones above the hill.

Later, I reach a room, where the moon stares
Cobwebbed through the window. The tide has ebbed,
Boats are careened in the harbour. Here is a bed.

Girl at the Seaside

I lean on a lighthouse rock
Where the seagowns flow,
A trawler slips from the dock
Sailing years ago.

Wine, tobacco and seamen
Cloud the green air,
A head of snakes in the rain
Talks away desire.

A sailor kisses me
Tasting of mackerel,
I analyse misery
Till mass bells peal.

I wait for clogs on the cobbles,
Dead feet at night,
Only a tempest blows
Darkness on sealight.

I've argued myself here
To the blue cliff-tops:
I'll drop through the sea-air
Till everything stops.

The Poet on the Island

TO THEODORE ROETHKE

On a wet night, laden with books for luggage,
And stumbling under the burden of himself,
He reached the pier, looking for a refuge.

Darkly he crossed to the island six miles off:
The engine pulsed, the sails invented rhythm,
While the sea expanded and the rain drummed softly.

Safety on water, he rocked with a new theme:
And in the warmth of his mind's greenhouse bloomed
A poem nurtured like a chrysanthemum.

His forehead, a Prussian helmet, moody, domed,
Relaxed in the sun: a lyric was his lance.
To be loved by the people, he, a stranger, hummed

In the herring-store on Sunday crammed with drunks
Ballads of bawdry with a speakeasy stress.
Yet lonely they left him, 'one of the Yanks.'

The children understood. This was not madness.
How many orphans had he fathered in words
Robust and cunning, but never heartless.

He watched the harbour scouted by sea-birds:
His fate was like fish under poetry's beaks:
Words began weirdly to take off inwards.

Time that they calendar in seasons not in clocks,
In gardens dug over and houses roofed,
Was to him a see-saw of joys and shocks,

Where his body withered but his style improved.
A storm shot up, his glass cracked in a gale:
An abstract thunder of darkness deafened

The listeners he'd once given roses, now hail.
He'd burst the lyric barrier: logic ended.
Doctors were called, and he agreed to sail.

(1 6 9)

The Scales of the Eyes

a poem in the form of a text and variations

I

To fleece the Fleece from golden sheep,
Or prey, or get—is it not lewd
That we be eaten by our food
And slept by sleepers in our sleep?

II

Sleep in the zero, sleep in the spore
Beyond the fires of Orion's hair,
Hard by the spiral burning dust;
Time being Always going west,
Let it be your dream.

Sleep sound in the spaceless lost
Curve running a blind coast;
Number and name, stretch the line
Out on the liquid of the brain,
Begin a falling dream.

The eye will flower in your night
A monstrous bulb, the broth of light
Stew in the marshes of a star;
Death is the wages of what you are,
Life is your long dream.

III

Around the city where I live
Dead men in their stone towns
Wait out the weather lying down,
And spread widely underground
The salt vines of blood.

Trains run a roaming sound
Under the wired shine of sun and rain.
Black sticks stand up in the sky
Where the wild rails cross and sprawl
Fast and still.

Out there beyond the island
The sea pounds a free way through,
Her wide tides spread on the sand
Stick and brine and rolling stone
The long weather long.

IV

Beneath my foot the secret beast
Whispers, and its stone sinews
Tremble with strength. In the dark earth
Iron winds its tangled nerves,
And the worm eats of the rock
There by the old waters.

Down in dark the rich comb
Gathers wrath out of the light,
The dead ploughed down in their graves
Record the canceled seed its doom.
City, white lion among waters,
Who settest thy claw upon the time,

Measure the tape, wind the clock,
Keep track of weather, watch water
And the work of trains. The bees hum
The honeyed doom of time and time
Again, and riddle this underground
How sweetness comes from the great strength.

V

a can of Dutch Cleanser

The blind maid shaking a stick,
Chasing dirt endlessly around
A yellow wall, was the very she
To violate my oldest nights;
I frighten of her still.

(1 7 1)

Her faceless bonnet flaps in wind
I cannot feel, she rages on,
The mad Margery of my sleep;
The socks wrinkle about her shoes
As she drats a maiden dream.

So shines her bleached virginity
On underground conveniences
That roar at once in porcelain hunger;
Her anger leaves me without stain
And white grits in the tub.

VI

The angry voice has sought me out,
Loud-speakers shout among the trees.
What use to hide? He made it all,
Already old when I began.

He held it all upon his knee
And spoke it soft in a big voice
Not so much loud as everywhere,
And all things had to answer him.

This world is not my oyster, nor
No slow socratic pearl grows here.
But the blind valves are closing
On only one grain of sand.

VII

The low sky was mute and white
And the sun a white hole in the sky
That morning when it came on to snow;
The hushed flakes fell all day.

The hills were hidden in a white air
And every bearing went away,
Landmarks being but white and white
For anyone going anywhere.

All lines were lost, a noon bell
I heard sunk in a sullen pool
Miles off. And yet this patient snow,
When later I walked out in it,

Had lodged itself in tips of grass
And made its mantle bridging so
It lay upon the air and not the earth
So light it hardly bent a blade.

VIII

From the road looking to the hill I saw
One hollow house hunched in the shoulder.
Windows blinded in a level sun
Stared with not random malice,
Though I had not been in that place.

But I have seen, at the white shore,
The crab eaten in the house of self
And the torn dog shark gutted in sand;
The whole sky goes white with silence
And bears on a few brazen flies.

As though the ground sighed under the foot
And the heart refused its blood; there is
No place I do not taste again
When I choke back the deeper sleep
Beneath the mined world I walk.

IX

Striding and turning, the caged sea
Knocks at the stone and falls away,
Will not rest night or day
Pacing to be free.

The spiral shell, held at the ear,
Hums the ocean or the blood
A distant cry, misunderstood
Of the mind in the coiled air.

X

Roads lead to the sea, and then?
The signs drown in the blowing sand,
The breathing and smoothing tide.
It has been a long journey so far.
Gull, where do I go now?

No matter what girls have been laid
In this sand, or far-wandering birds
Died here, I think I will not know
What no galling road has told,
Why to be here or how.

Question the crab, the wasted moon,
The spume blown of the smashed wave,
Ask Polaris about the fish.
No good. I would go home, but there is
No way to go but back.

XI

Plunged the tunnel with the wet wall
Through, sounding with sea space
And the shaken earth, I fell below
The shark diving and the wry worm.
Blindly I nudged a gasping sky.

Against drowning to be born in a caul
Is well. But all free engines
Race to burn themselves out, tear up
The earth and the air and choke on a mouth
Of dirt, throwing their oil.

In long halls of hospital, the white
Eye peeled beneath the pool of light;
Then the blinded, masked and stifled sky
Screamed silver when it grated bone
Beaching a stained keel.

But at last the moon swung dark and away
And waters withered to a salt.
Parched and shaken on a weaned world
I was in wonder burning cold
And in darkness did rest.

XII

In the water cave, below the root,
The blind fish knew my veins.
I heard ticking the water drop,
The sighing where the wind fell,
When the bat laddered the black air.

(174)

Chalk and bone and salt and stone.
Let mother water begin me again,
For I am blackened with burning, gone
From the vain fire of the air,
The one salamander weather.

Slow cold salt, weeds washed
Under crumbling rock ledges
In the water cave below the root,
Quiet the crystal in the dark,
Let the blind way shine out.

XIII

Gone the armies on the white roads,
The priests blessing and denouncing,
Gone the aircraft speaking power
Through the ruined and echoing air;
And life and death are here.

The quiet pool, if you will listen,
Hisses with your blood, winds
Together vine and vein and thorn,
The thin twisted threads red
With the rust of breath.

Now is the hour in the wild garden
Grown blessed. Tears blinding the eyes,
The martyr's wound and the hurt heart
Seal and are dumb, the ram waits
In the thicket of nerves.

XIV

In the last hour of the dream
The eye turned upon itself
And stood at bay, peering among
The salt fibers of its blood.

String of the cradle and the kite,
Vine twisted against the bone,
Salt tears washing the sinews,
The spider strangled in her web.

(1 7 5)

I stood in the last wilderness
Watching the grass at the sea's edge
Bend as to the breathing touch
Of a blind slither at the stalk.

String of the navel and the net,
Vein threading the still pool,
Dumb fingers in the wet sand
Where the heart bled its secret food.

Salt of the flesh, I knew the world
For the white veil over the eye,
The eye for the caged water of light;
The beast asleep in the bleeding snare.

xv

And the rabbis have said the last word
And the iron gates they have slammed shut
Closing my body from the world.
Around me all Long Island lies
Smouldering and still.

Cold winter, the roller coasters
Stand in the swamps by the sea, and bend
The lizards of their bones alone,
August of lust and the hot dog
Frozen in their fat.

But the sea goes her own way.
Around and down her barren green
Sliding and sucking the cold flesh
Of the wrinkled world, with no bone
To such mother-makings.

I have sept through the wide seine.
From Coney Island to Phlegethon
Is no great way by ferris wheel,
And we informal liquors may
Easily despise your bones.

XVI

Snow on the beaches, briny ice,
Grass white and cracking with the cold.
The light is from the ocean moon
Hanging in the dead height.

Gull rises in the snowy marsh
A shale of light flaked from a star,
The white hair of the breaking wave
Splashed the night sky.

Down at the root, in the warm dream,
The lily bows among the ruins.
Kingdoms rise and are blown down
While the summer fly hums.

XVII

When black water breaks the ice
The moon is milk and chalk of tooth.
The star is bleeding in the still pool
And the horny skin is left behind
When journey must be new-begun.

Teiresias watching in the wood
A wheel of snakes, gave his sight
To know the coupled work of time,
How pale woman and fiery man
Married their disguise away.

Then all was the self, but self was none;
Knowing itself in the fiery dark
The blind pool of the eye became
The sailing of the moon and sun
Through brightness melted into sky.

XVIII

Of leaf and branch and rain and light,
The spider's web glistered with wet,
The robin's breast washed red in sun
After the rapid storm goes on;

Of long light level on the lake
And white on the side of lonely houses,
The thunder going toward the hill,
The last lightning cracking the sky;

New happiness of everything!
The blind worm lifts up his head
And the sparrow shakes a wet wing
In the home of little while.

The Goose Fish

On the long shore, lit by the moon
To show them properly alone,
Two lovers suddenly embraced
So that their shadows were as one.
The ordinary night was graced
For them by the swift tide of blood
That silently they took at flood,
And for a little time they prized
    Themselves emparadised.

Then, as if shaken by stage-fright
Beneath the hard moon's bony light,
They stood together on the sand
Embarrassed in each other's sight
But still conspiring hand in hand,
Until they saw, there underfoot,
As though the world had found them out,
The goose fish turning up, though dead,
    His hugely grinning head.

There in the china light he lay,
Most ancient and corrupt and grey
They hesitated at his smile,
Wondering what it seemed to say
To lovers who a little while
Before had thought to understand,
By violence upon the sand,

The only way that could be known
    To make a world their own.

It was a wide and moony grin
Together peaceful and obscene;
They knew not what he would express,
So finished a comedian
He might mean failure or success,
But took it for an emblem of
Their sudden, new and guilty love
To be observed by, when they kissed,
    That rigid optimist.

So he became their patriarch,
Dreadfully mild in the half-dark.
His throat that the sand seemed to choke,
His picket teeth, these left their mark
But never did explain the joke
That so amused him, lying there
While the moon went down to disappear
Along the still and tilted track
    That bears the zodiac.

Lot Later

VAUDEVILLE FOR GEORGE FINKEL

I

It seems now far off and foolish, a memory
Torn at the hem from the fabric of a dream
In drunken sleep, but why was I the one?
God knows, there were no fifty righteous, nor
Ten righteous, in town just at that very moment;
Gone south for the winter, maybe. And moreover,
I wouldn't have been one of the ten or fifty
Or whatever, if there had been. Abraham
Stood up to Him, but not for me—more likely
For the principle of the thing. I've always been
Honest enough for this world, and respected

(1 7 9)

In this town—but to be taken by the hair
Like that, and lifted into that insane story,
Then to be dropped when it was done with me . . .
I tell you, I felt *used*.

                    In the first place,
I never knew the two of them were angels:
No wings, no radiance. I thought they might be students
Going from town to town, seeing the country.
I said "Come in the house, we'll have a drink,
Some supper, why not stay the night?" They did.
The only oddity was they didn't bother
With evening prayers, and that made me suspect
They might be Somebody. But in my home town
It doesn't take much; before I thought it out
People were coming round beating the door:
"Who you got in the house, let's have a party."
It was a pretty nice town in those days,
With always something going on, a dance
Or a big drunk with free women, or boys
For those who wanted boys, in the good weather
We used to play strip poker in the yard.
But just then, when I looked at those young gents,
I had a notion it was not the time,
And shouted through the door, "Go home, we're tired."
Nobody went. But all these drunks began
To pound the door and throw rocks at the windows
And make suggestions as to what they might do
When they got hold of the two pretty young men.
Matters were getting fairly desperate
By this time, and I said to those outside,
"Look, I got here my two daughters, virgins
Who never been there yet. I send them out,
Only my guests should have a peaceful night."
That's how serious the situation was.
Of course it wasn't the truth about the kids,
Who were both married, and, as a matter of fact,
Not much better than whores, and both the husbands
Knocking their horns against the chandeliers
Of my own house—but still, it's what I said.
It got a big laugh out there, and remarks,
Till the two young men gave me a nice smile
And stretched out one hand each, and suddenly
It got pitch dark outside, people began

Bumping into each other and swearing; then
They cleared away and everything was quiet.
So one young man opens his mouth, he says,
"You've got till sunrise, take the wife and kids
And the kids' husbands, and go. Go up to the hills."
The other says, "The Lord hath sent us to
Destroy this place" and so forth and so forth.
You can imagine how I felt. I said,
"Now look, now after all . . ." and my wife said,
"Give me a few days till I pack our things,"
And one of them looked at his watch and said,
"It's orders, lady, sorry, you've got till dawn."
I said, "Respectfully, gentlemen, but who
Lives in the hills? I've got to go, so why
Shouldn't I go to Zoar, which is a nice
Town with a country club which doesn't exclude
Jews?" "So go to Zoar if you want," they said.
"Whatever you do, you shouldn't look back here."
We argued all night long. First this, then that.
My son-in-laws got into the act: "You're kidding,
Things of this nature simply do not happen
To people like us." I said, "These here are angels,
But suit yourselves." The pair of them said, "We'll stay,
Only deed us the house and furniture."
"I wouldn't deed you a dead fish," I said,
"Besides, I'm going to take the girls along."
"So take," they said, "they weren't such a bargain."
The two visitors all this time said nothing,
They might as well not have been there. But I
Believed what I was told, and this, I think,
Makes all the difference—between life and death,
I mean—to feel sincerely that there's truth
In something, even if it's God knows what.
My poor old woman felt it too, that night,
She only couldn't hold it to the end.
The girls just packed their biggest pocketbooks
With candy and perfume; they'd be at home
Most anywhere, even in a hill.

                    At last
I knelt down and I spoke to my God as follows:
"Dear Sir," I said, "I do not understand
Why you are doing this to my community,

And I do not understand why, doing it,
You let me out. There's only this onething,
So help me, that with all my faults I do
Believe you are able to do whatever you say
You plan to do. Myself, I don't belong
In any operation on this scale.
I've always been known here as a nice fellow,
Which is low enough to be or want to be:
Respectfully I ask to be let go
To live out my declining years at peace
In Zoar with my wife and the two kids
Such as they are. A small house will do.
Only I shouldn't be part of history."
Of course no one answered. One of them said:
"If you're about through, please get on your feet,
It's time to go." My daughters' gorgeous husbands
Were drinking on the porch before we left.

II

My relative Abraham saw it happen: the whole
Outfit went up in smoke, he said. One minute
There was the town, with banks and bars and grills
And the new sewage disposal plant, all looking
(he said) terribly innocent in the first light;
Then it ignited. It went. All those old pals
Gone up, or maybe down. I am his nephew,
Maybe you know, he had troubles himself,
With the maid, and his own son. That's neither here
Nor there. We'd been forbidden to look, of course,
But equally of course my old girl had to look.
She turned around, and in one minute there
She was, a road sign or a mileage marker.
By this time, though, I knew that what we were in
Was very big, and I told the kids Come on.
We didn't stop to cry, even. Also
We never went to Zoar. I began to think
How real estate was high, how I'd been told
To go up in the hills, and how I'd always
Wanted to live in the country, a gentleman
Like Abraham, maybe, and have my flocks
Or whatever you call them—herds. Well, I found out.
A cave, we lived in, a real cave, out of rock.
I envied those bums my son-in-laws, until

I remembered they were dead. And the two girls,
My nutsy kids, getting the odd idea
That the whole human race had been destroyed
Except for us, conceived—this word I love,
Conceived—the notion that they should be known
In carnal union by their poppa. Me.
Poor dear old Dad. Most any man might dream
About his daughters; darling and stupid chicks
As these ones were, I'd dreamed, even in daytime,
Such brilliant dreams. But they? They bought some booze,
Having remembered to bring money along.
Something I never thought of, considering
I was in the hand of God, and got me boiled.
And then—I'm told—on two successive nights
Arrived on my plain stone couch and—what shall I say?
Had me? I was completely gone at the time,
And have no recollection. But there they were,
The pair of them, at the next moon, knocked up,
And properly, and by their Dad. The kids
Turned out to be boys, Moab and Ben-Ammi
By name. I have been given to understand
On competent authority that they will father
A couple of peoples known as Moabites
And Ammonites, distinguished chiefly by
Heathenish ways and ignorance of the Law.
And I did this? Or this was done to me,
A foolish man who lived in the grand dream
One instant, at the fuse of miracle and
The flare of light, a man no better than most,
Who loves the Lord and does not know His ways,
Neither permitted the pleasure of his sins
Nor punished for them, and whose aging daughters
Bring him his supper nights, and clean the cave.

Arrival: The Capital

After the five hour flight the confusion
  Of stepping out to shake hands with the past.
No one to meet since nobody knows.
                             Almost a foreigner,
Without excitement, with no apology, I break
Over scuttled faces crowding the barrier.

Secure as a diplomat in the taxi's corner I slide
Through the suburban morning
  Watching for changes,
                  suspended like limbo.

Just as one left it. Children carrying bundles
Or leaning dirty over the river wall. Mothers
Strealing. Fronded canals clotted. Young men,
Idle, backs to street-corners, talk unemployment,
                          emigration.

The city now, at its center,
The years between us like ectoplasm.

          My train down the country
And home, not leaving 'till evening,
I tally old haunts, methodically—
              like one walks stones
In a familiar, abandoned churchyard:
The scrawn rake pigeons; the same skin-dry men
In prewar topcoats (kippers for lunch
In empty briefcases) gently speaking aloud
To themselves.
            Countrymen up the day
From the provinces to sales or the football.
"The enormous tragedy of the dream
            in the peasants' bent shoulders."
Down by the freighterless docks and the Custom House
The old characters still sitting alone in the sunlight—

                      (1 8 4)

Bearded, in spectacles, old age and rags,
Great sacks of books. Reading. A part of salvation
In private exile.
                        Her dog by the lamppost on Wicklow Street
That crone woman still playing her harp,
But now to herself. Her husband,
And with him *his* harp, has departed.
                              Indifferent students
Coming from lectures or sitting about
On the Green; a new generation
                    avoiding old problems.
At intervals, shiftyeyed scroungers in colourless clothes
Hang around public urinals
                        and girls' school exits.
     Out at suburban seasides I know
Whitecollar workers on holiday, trousers
Up to their knees, paddle children
In rusty salt water.
                        Along the seafront wall
In faded deckchairs, basking nuns
Drain little warmth from a watery sun.
                              And weaving,
Like some geological fault, through it all
Those in control and responsible
              leaving well enough alone.
In public bars professors and such, in late
Middle age, on their own, stare over whiskey thinking
Nothing in particular, considering
Everything in general. Waiting.
                  Nothing of matter will happen.
About them, unheeded, the old conversation.
                                    Down
In that prominent corner, the flies
Of his trousers unproperly buttoned,
Grey hair sticking from under his soft hat
Like black sheep's wool, a national poet.
              I remember
An old poem beginning:
                        "If I went away
I should never come back."
Somewhere outside in their building-scheme lives
Old friends are respectably settled.

(1 8 5)

I finish my drink and leave for the train
Home to my provincial town
                     having spoken to no one.

CHARLES OLSON

Maximus, to Himself

I have had to learn the simplest things
last. Which made for difficulties.
Even at sea I was slow, to get the hand out, or to cross
a wet deck.
              The sea was not, finally, my trade.
But even my trade, at it, I stood estranged
from that which was most familiar. Was delayed,
and not content with the man's argument
that such postponement
is now the nature of
obedience,
              that we are all late
              in a slow time,
              that we grow up many
              And the single
              is not easily
              known

It could be, though the sharpness (the *achiote*)
I note in others,
makes more sense
than my own distances. The agilities

              they show daily
              who do the world's
              businesses

(1 8 6)

And who do nature's
as I have no sense
I have done either

I have made dialogues,
have discussed ancient texts,
have thrown what light I could, offered
what pleasures
doceat allows

But the known?
This, I have had to be given,
a life, love, and from one man
the world.

Tokens.
But sitting here
I look out as a wind
and water man, testing
And missing
some proof

I know the quarters
of the weather, where it comes from,
where it goes. But the stem of me,
this I took from their welcome,
or their rejection, of me

And my arrogance
was neither diminished
nor increased,
by the communication

2

It is undone business
I speak of, this morning,
with the sea
stretching out
from my feet

Maximus, to Gloucester, Letter 19
(A Pastoral Letter

    relating
    to the care of souls,
    it says)

          He had smiled at us,
          each time we were in town, inquired
          how the baby was, had two cents
          for the weather, wore
          (besides his automobile)
          good clothes.
                    And a pink face.

          It was yesterday
          it all came out. The gambit
          (as he crossed the street,
          after us): "I don't believe
          I know your name." Given.
          How do you do,
          how do you do. And then:
          "Pardon me, but
          what church
          do you belong to,
          may I ask?"

And the whole street, the town, the cities, the nation
blinked, in the afternoon sun, as the gun
was held at them. And I wavered
in the thought.

          I sd, you may, sir.
          He sd, what, sir.
          I sd, none,
          sir.

And the light was back.
For I am no merchant.
Nor so young I need to take a stance
to a loaded
smile.

I have known the face
of God.
And turned away,
turned,
as He did,
his backside

2

And now it is noon
of a cloudy sunday.
And a bird sings
loudly

And my daughter, naked
on the porch, sings
as best she can, and loudly,
back

She wears her own face
as we do not,
until we cease to wear
the clouds
of all confusion,

of all confusers
who wear the false face
He never wore, Whose
is terrible. Is
perfection

The Moon Is the Number 18

is a monstrance,
the blue dogs bay,
and the son sits,
grieving

is a grinning god, is
the mouth of, is
the dripping moon

while in the tower the cat
preens
and all motion
is a crab

and there is nothing he can do but what they do, watch
the face of waters, and fire

> The blue dogs paw,
> lick the droppings, dew
> or blood, whatever
> results are. And night,
> the crab, rays round
> attentive as the cat to catch
> human sound

> The blue dogs rue,
> as he does, as he would howl, confronting
> the wind which rocks what was her, while prayers
> striate the snow, words blow
> as questions cross fast, fast
> as flames, as flames form, melt
> along any darkness

Birth is an instance as is a host, namely, death

The moon has no air

> In the red tower
> in that tower where she also sat
> in that particular tower where watching & moving
>   are,
> there,
> there where what triumph there is, is: there
> is all substance, all creature
> all there is against the dirty moon, against
> number, image, sortilege—

> alone with cat & crab,
> and sound is, is, his
> conjecture

Two Views of a Cadaver Room

1

The day she visited the dissecting room
They had four men laid out, black as burnt turkey,
Already half unstrung. A vinegary fume
Of the death vats clung to them;
The white-smocked boys started working.
The head of his cadaver had caved in,
And she could scarcely make out anything
In that rubble of skull plates and old leather.
A sallow piece of string held it together.

In their jars the snail-nosed babies moon and glow.
He hands her the cut-out heart like a cracked heirloom.

2

In Brueghel's panorama of smoke and slaughter
Two people only are blind to the carrion army:
He, afloat in the sea of her blue satin
Skirts, sings in the direction
Of her bare shoulder, while she bends,
Fingering a leaflet of music, over him,
Both of them deaf to the fiddle in the hands
Of the death's-head shadowing their song.
These Flemish lovers flourish; not for long.

Yet desolation, stalled in paint, spares the little country
Foolish, delicate, in the lower right-hand corner.

Suicide off Egg Rock

Behind him the hotdogs split and drizzled
On the public grills, and the ochreous salt flats,
Gas tanks, factory stacks—that landscape
Of imperfections his bowels were part of—

(1 9 1)

Rippled and pulsed in the glassy updraft.
Sun struck the water like a damnation.
No pit of shadow to crawl into,
And his blood beating the old tattoo
I am, I am, I am. Children
Were squealing where combers broke and the spindrift
Raveled wind-ripped from the crest of the wave.
A mongrel working his legs to a gallop
Hustled a gull flock to flap off the sandspit.

He smoldered, as if stone-deaf, blindfold,
His body beached with the sea's garbage,
A machine to breathe and beat forever.
Flies filing in through a dead skate's eyehole
Buzzed and assailed the vaulted brainchamber.
The words in his book wormed off the pages.
Everything glittered like blank paper.

Everything shrank in the sun's corrosive
Ray but Egg Rock on the blue wastage.
He heard when he walked into the water

The forgetful surf creaming on those ledges.

Daddy

You do not do, you do not do
Any more, black shoe
In which I have lived like a foot
For thirty years, poor and white,
Barely daring to breathe or Achoo!

Daddy, I have had to kill you.
You died before I had time—
Marble-heavy, a bag full of God,
Ghastly statue with one grey toe
Big as a Frisco seal

And a head in the freakish Atlantic
Where it pours bean green over blue
In the waters off beautiful Nauset.
I used to pray to recover you.
Ach, du!

In the German tongue, in the Polish town
Scraped flat by the roller
Of wars, wars, wars.
But the name of the town is common.
My Polack friend

Says there are a dozen or two.
So I never could tell where you
Put your foot, your root,
I never could talk to you.
The tongue stuck in my jaw.

It stuck in a barb wire snare.
Ich, ich, ich, ich!
I could hardly speak.
I thought every German was you.
And the language obscene

An engine, an engine
Chuffing me off like a Jew.
A Jew to Dachau, Auschwitz, Belsen.
I began to talk like a Jew.
I think I may well be a Jew.

The snows of the Tyrol, the clear beer of Vienna
Are not very pure or true.
With my gypsy ancestress and my weird luck
And my Tarot pack and my Tarot pack
I may be a bit of a Jew.

I have always been scared of *you*,
With your Luftwaffe, your gobbledygoo.
And your neat moustache
And your Aryan eye, bright blue.
Panzer-man, panzer-man, o You!

(*1 9 3*)

Not God but a swastika
So black no sky could squeak through.
Every woman adores a Fascist,
The boot in the face, the brute
Brute heart of a brute like you.

You stand at the blackboard, daddy,
In the picture I have of you,
A cleft in your chin instead of your foot
But no less a devil for that, no not
Any less the black man who

Bit my pretty red heart in two.
I was ten when they buried you.
At twenty I tried to die
And get back, back, back to you.
I thought even the bones would do.

But they pulled me out of the sack,
And they stuck me together with glue.
And then I knew what to do.
I made a model of you,
A man in black with a Meinkampf look

And a love of the rack and the screw.
And I said I do, I do.
So daddy, I'm finally through.
The black telephone's off at the root,
The voices just can't worm through.

If I've killed one man, I've killed two—
The vampire who said he was you
And drank my blood for a year—
Seven years, if you want to know.
Daddy, you can lie back now.

There's a stake in your fat black heart
And the villagers never liked you.
They are dancing and stamping on you.
They always *knew* it was you.
Daddy, daddy, you bastard, I'm through.

Ariel

Stasis in darkness.
Then the substanceless blue
Pour of tor and distances.

God's lioness,
How one we grow,
Pivot of heels and knees!—The furrow

Splits and passes, sister to
The brown arc
Of the neck I cannot catch,

Nigger-eye
Berries cast dark
Hooks—

Black sweet blood mouthfuls,
Shadows.
Something else

Hauls me through air—
Thighs, hair;
Flakes from my heels.

White
Godiva, I unpeel—
Dead hands, dead stringencies.

And now I
Foam to wheat, a glitter of seas.
The child's cry

Melts in the wall.
And I
Am the arrow,

The dew that flies
Suicidal, at one with the drive
Into the red

Eye, the cauldron of morning.

(1 9 5)

Fever 103°

Pure? What does it mean?
The tongues of hell
Are dull, dull as the triple

Tongues of dull, fat Cerberus
Who wheezes at the gate. Incapable
Of licking clean

The aguey tendon, the sin, the sin.
The tinder cries.
The indelible smell

Of a snuffed candle!
Love, love, the low smokes roll
From me like Isadora's scarves, I'm in a fright

One scarf will catch and anchor in the wheel,
Such yellow sullen smokes
Make their own element. They will not rise,

But trundle round the globe
Choking the aged and the meek,
The weak

Hothouse baby in its crib,
The ghastly orchid
Hanging its hanging garden in the air,

Devilish leopard!
Radiation turned it white
And killed it in an hour.

Greasing the bodies of adulterers
Like Hiroshima ash and eating in.
The sin. The sin.

Darling, all night
I have been flickering, off, on, off, on.
The sheets grow heavy as a lecher's kiss.

Three days. Three nights.
Lemon water, chicken
Water, water makes me retch.

I am too pure for you or anyone.
Your body
Hurts me as the world hurts God. I am a lantern—

My head a moon
Of Japanese paper, my gold beaten skin
Infinitely delicate and infinitely expensive.

Does not my heat astound you! And my light!
All by myself I am a huge camellia
Glowing and coming and going, flush on flush.

I think I am going up,
I think I may rise—
The heads of hot metal fly, and I love, I

Am a pure acetylene
Virgin
Attended by roses,

By kisses, by cherubim,
By whatever these pink things mean!
Not you, nor him

Nor him, nor him
(My selves dissolving, old whore petticoats)—
To Paradise.

The Smell on the Landing

Where the decay begins, the sun
Through barred windows
Falls to its knees. We turn
The key two floors below
And walk towards the smell:
It is not the smell of death
Or of violence or even of Hell;
It is the odour of having no hope,
Of lying late, of being itself alone.

Trapped on the landing, a sea
Of cabbage air is pushed
To furrows with the turning key.
The tower collapses, rushed
Past the falling flower and its sound;
We retch involuntarily,
For our stomachs have found
The common taste of filth,
We are the thinking flesh left on its own.

One family lives in the one room
Whose door is never open,
But the wireless and children quietly boom
Alive behind its walls; when
Armageddon on the stairs
Muffles the company and steals
A winding whisper through its ears,
Then can all the eaten meals
And dirty clothes come into their own.

On the street it is flag day—a flag
For a coin is conscious charity,
But here where charity begins,
A Home is home enough to be
Our street of Victorian fronts,

Our refuge from the acid rain,
So we may hurry from the yellow fog
To the dead life on our stairs once
More ourselves in ourselves alone.

Annotations of Auschwitz

(I)

When the burnt flesh is finally at rest,
The fires in the asylum grates will come up
And wicks turn down to darkness in the madman's eyes.

(II)

My suit is hairy, my carpet smells of death,
My toothbrush handle grows a cuticle.
I have six million foulnesses of breath
Am I mad? The doctor holds my testicles
While the room fills with the zyklon B I cough.

(III)

On Picadilly underground I fall asleep—
I shuffle with the naked to the steel door,
Now I am only ten from the front—I wake up—
We are past Gloucester Rd., I am not a Jew,
But scratches web the ceiling of the train.

(IV)

Around staring buildings the pale flowers grow;
The frenetic butterfly, the bee made free by work,
Rouse and rape the pollen pads, the nectar stoops.
The rusting railway ends here. The blind end in Europe's gut.
Touch one piece of unstrung barbed wire—
Let it taste blood: let one man scream in pain,
Death's Botanical Gardens can flower again.

(V)

A man eating his dressing in the hospital
Is lied to by his stomach. It's a final feast to him
Of beef, blood pudding and black bread.

(*1 9 9*)

The orderly can't bear to see this mimic face
With its prim accusing picture after death.
On the stiff square a thousand bodies
Dig up useless ground—he hates them all,
These lives ignoble as ungoverned glands.
They fatten in statistics everywhere
And with their sick, unkillable fear of death
They crowd out peace from executioners' sleep.

(VI)

Forty thousand bald men drowning in a stream—
The like of light on all those bobbing skulls
Has never been seen before. Such death, says the painter,
Is worthwhile—it makes a colour never known.
It makes a sight that's unimagined, says the poet.
It's nothing to do with me, says the man who hates
The poet and the painter. Six million deaths can hardly
Occur at once. What do they make? Perhaps
An idiot's normalcy. I need never feel afraid
When I salt the puny snail—cruelty's grown up
And waits for time and men to bring into its hands
The snail's adagio and all the taunting life
Which has not cared about or guessed its tortured scope.

(VII)

London is full of chickens on electric spits,
    Cooking in windows where the public pass.
This, say the chickens, is their Auschwitz,
    And all poultry eaters are psychopaths.

(2 0 0)

FROM *A Sky of Late Summer*

The fountains of fire
Play in the deep sky
Their wild becoming,
Spray upon spray.

Will the fountains of August
Be held by the names
Of a child's beasts
In the glistering cage?

By secret numbers
Drawn from the fire?
But how the night trembles
Star upon star!

So the wild light
Arches and falls
And the fountains of language
Arch, fall,

Until stirred with no word
The deep heart
Far beneath its own fountain
Unspent though spent far

Lifts with a cry
To the heart of that fire
And cries no name
But is named in the pure

Flaming that utters
The visible flame,
Breath of all naming,
Speech of each name:

(2 0 1)

Is! Is!
Bursting to spell
The words and the names
In the blessing spilled

Star after star,
Spray upon spray:
The deep midnight's
Perpetual day.

Promise Your Hand

Promise your hand, the dawn is yet slow
And I am spun through ten years'
Seas and cities. Uncertain trees
Pursue the road; and though I take
The next train, draw the shade,
Names not in my language
Beat at the window, cold enemies
Sit opposite, masked
In the local headlines, their wine and bread
Not for my asking. They
Lurch and wind among the dark
Mountains. I am searched at the frontier,
Walled in grey uniforms, I am flung
To the high unwanted room to count
My foreign coins like minutes, with the bent
Concierge watching from the hall
Wishing me neither good nor harm
Wishing me nothing. Look, the vague trees
Clutch even here, not yet so tall
But clutching. Promise your hand,
I will speed these rails again, leap
By these lights, hide between cars,
But be, only be the patient and sure
Miracle of yourself at the last far station,
Implausible point on the wild map
Suddenly real and from what great arc
Marvelously catching my flight; containing me.

(2 0 2)

PETER REDGROVE

Against Death

We are glad to have birds in our roof
Sealed off from rooms by white ceiling,
And glad to glimpse them homing straight
Blinking across the upstairs windows,
And to listen to them scratching on the laths
As we bed and whisper staring at the ceiling.
We're glad to be hospitable to birds.
In our rooms, in general only humans come,
We keep no cats and dislike wet-mouthed dogs,
And wind comes up the floorboards in a gale,
So then we keep to bed: no more productive place
To spend a blustery winter evening and keep warm.
Occasionally a spider capsises in the bath,
Blot streaming with legs among the soap,
Cool and scab-bodied, soot-and-suet,
So we have to suffocate it down the pipe
For none of us'd have dealings with it,
Like kissing a corpse's lips, even
Through the fingers, so I flood it out.
In our high-headed rooms we're going to breed
Many human beings for their home
To fill the house with children and with life,
Running in service of the shrill white bodies,
With human life but for sparrows in the roof,
Wiping noses and cleaning up behind,
Slapping and sympathising, and catching glimpses
Of each other and ourselves as we were then,
And let out in the world a homing of adults.
And if there ever should be a corpse in the house
Hard on its bedsprings in a room upstairs,
Smelling of brass-polish, with sucked-in cheeks,
Staring through eyelids at a scratching ceiling,
Some firm'd hurry it outdoors and burn it quick—
We'd expect no more to happen to ourselves
Our children gradually foregoing grief of us
As the hot bodies of the sparrows increase each summer.

(203)

For No Good Reason

I walk on the waste-ground for no good reason
Except that fallen stones and cracks
Bulging with weed suit my mood
Which is gloomy, irascible, selfish, among the split timbers
Of somebody's home, and the bleached rags of wallpaper.
My trouser-legs pied with water-drops,
I knock a sparkling rain from hemlock-polls,
I crash a puddle up my shin,
Brush a nettle across my hand,
And swear—then sweat from what I said:
Indeed, the sun withdraws as if I stung.

Indeed, she withdrew as if I stung,
And I walk up and down among these canted beams, bricks
        and scraps,
Bitten walls and weed-stuffed gaps
Looking as it would feel now, if I walked back,
Across the carpets of my home, my own home.

Dismissal

She dismisses me in late sunbeams
In the meadow mealy with life.
Pollens, smoking, mingle,
All the thin flowers shuffle,
Stagger with rummaging throngs.
I am attentive to my sentence,
Attention is my mask;
I march to the fringe of the wood.

My feeling is worn out.
She fidgets like a husk
Blown askance in a web of hair,
Pale, frowning and white-necked.
My step just clips a bee
Which sizzles, and plucks free.

Thick roots strap the soil.
I trash mushrooms at each step
That were not there last night
White-headed and wry-necked.
A husk on a gossamer
Snaps across my sight,
Gibbets on my wink,
And I catch through gasps in the leaves
As the sun couches on breeze
All the small clouds like thin masks
Shucking lightly into dark.

New Forms

I see all this new matter of the snow
Across this window, how it limps
Gently along and down, not like
A snow-storm or tempest, but like breeding.
And a light wind takes it gently with new shapes
And pats and moulds over the last new shapes
Of cricked branch and jagged verge,
Over tallow and bosses of the first ice
And greybeard stubble and thronging bracken of the first frost—
How it bats, bounces, tosses, scribbles, flings, cancels,
Writes out afresh round the wall of the house
In settled draughts unsettled forms
Leaping and twinkling over the gates,
Like our thoughts of the unborn
Crowding the old light
Belly fringed and curving like an horizon.

Required of You This Night

A smoky sunset. I dab my eyes.
It stinks into the black wick of the wood.

Sparks wriggle, cut. I turn my back.
And night is at my frosty back.

I turn again. All stars!
It's bedtime.

There's no sky in my dreams, I dream none.
I work for sky, I work by sprinting up,
Breathing, sprinting up, and one star appears.

I chase it. It enlarges and I wake.
Dawn climbs into the sky like black smoke with white nails.

It's compact with the day's sharpness.
I'll dry my sopping pillow with it.
How long'll that take? I guess till sunset.

And then it sinks
All befrogged into that white glare.
The night is at my back instantly,
Draughty, and no star at all.
I weep again. I weep again frankly.
Sleep is nothing when you do it,
And nothing but a prim smile,
Except you're fighting to pull the sun down
That may not come unless you fight
Not for you anyway, Peter.

KENNETH REXROTH

A Sword in a Cloud of Light

Your hand in mine, we walk out
To watch the Christmas Eve crowds
On Fillmore Street, the Negro
District. The night is thick with

Frost. The people hurry, wreathed
In their smoky breaths. Before
The shop windows the children
Jump up and down with spangled
Eyes. Santa Clauses ring bells.
Cars stall and honk. Streetcars clang.
Loudspeakers on the lampposts
Sing carols, on jukeboxes
In the bars Louis Armstrong
Plays *White Christmas*. In the joints
The girls strip and grind and bump
To *Jingle Bells*. Overhead
The neon signs scribble and
Erase and scribble again
Messages of avarice,
Joy, fear, hygiene, and the proud
Names of the middle classes.
The moon beams like a pudding.
We stop at the main corner
And look up diagonally
Across, at the rising moon,
And the solemn, orderly
Vast winter constellations.
You say, "There's Orion!"
The most beautiful object
Either of us will ever
Know in the world or in life
Stands in the moonlit empty
Heavens, over the swarming
Men, women and children, black
And white, joyous and greedy,
Evil and good, buyer and
Seller, master and victim,
Like some immense theorem,
Which, if once solved would forever
Solve the mystery and pain
Under the bells and spangles.
There he is, the man of the
Night before Christmas, spread out
On the sky like a true god
In whom it would only be
Necessary to believe
A little. I am fifty

And you are five. It would do
No good to say this and it
May do no good to write it.
Believe in Orion. Believe
In the night, the moon, the crowded
Earth. Believe in Christmas and
Birthdays and Easter rabbits.
Believe in all those fugitive
Compounds of nature, all doomed
To waste away and go out.
Always be true to these things.
They are all there is. Never
Give up this savage religion
For the blood drenched civilized
Abstractions of the rascals
Who live by killing you and me.

ANNE RIDLER

Beads from Blackpool

In that town, nothing is sane but the sea.
Thank God, the waves still break all winter over the
Ice-cream caves and fairy grottoes, over the
Lavatory bricks, the scaffolds of flimsy fun,
Ring contempt through rungs of the pier, fling
Black spray among the crowds, orphaned of summer,
Who nose the shops and gaze at boards announcing
Epstein's *Jacob,* erotic displays, and oysters.
Thank God the sea is ruthless.
They might have thought to teach this lesson, who chose
Blackpool for Overseas Assembly—showing
The ugliness men love, the wisdom of divorce.
But we refused it, briefly met to part
In a curtainless room converted from a shop,
Parting in agony behind the plateglass window.

It went hard with us, went hard with others
More silent than we, more used to obey
In silent rebellion.
                          Was there good in this?
I make no judgement yet, nor judge for the rest;
The time is dark yet, I am yet uncertain
If I accept that parting.

After bodily death, is death rejected
By the still-living self—through all advance
Felt still as an outrage, only in glory
Alas only in glory to be understood?

Life in our hands, we grope again to each other.
By what sensible link? Amber beads
Bought in the shamming town—Beads from Blackpool
(The fiery kind, solid wine, or flame
Bound in the stone against all inward change,
Docile to change of light and to our possession).
Now the child, immanent then, well born
Now and six months old,
Sucks, and while I nourish her and cherish her,
Seizes the beads with vague violent fingers.
So men clutch at hope. The seas break
And fade, the parting is past and still unsolved,
The miles shudder between,
And the obstinate flame, lovelocked in a living palm,
Speaks of sequence, denies the absolute death.

Venetian Scene

S. Giorgio Maggiore

Fill the piazza with blue water
And gaze across domestic seas
From church to church. The tide is tame,
The streets look firm with floating marble.
Who made the sea ride in the city?
Movement is all a floating. Ride
The idle tide that smooths the steps:

Now statues ride in the blue air,
Light floats across the white facade
And seaweed over the marble stairs.

Making Love, Killing Time

The clock within us, speaking time
By heart-beat seconds and by mental years,
Is garrulous in any gear,
So life at once seems short and endless.
Who is not glad to find the hour later than he thought?
For so he has killed, not time
But the inward timing of the ceaseless rote.
Its beat, which makes him count the cost
Of that creation which, loving, he cannot resist,
Hurries him on to end whatever was begun—
The child, to be grown, the poem, to be done.

But in each other's arms,
Or on the tide of prayer, when we
Encountering souls support each other, like swimmers in a
        blissful sea,
The cost is known as the cause of bliss,
And the gabbling rote is heard as a murmur of peace.
So *making love* we say, but love makes us
Again to be as in our listening-time,
When hearing our heart-beat we took it for the world's,
And with no wish to escape it, then and there
Loved what we were.

Pan and Syrinx

Across the heavy sands running they came,
She like his shadow shot on before him,
But bit by bit it shortened to full stop
And noonday dot. Then, just within his grasp
She faded, in the sunburst of his joy
Expunged. He had not time to countermand
His smirk of pride, or blandly to run on
As if the running were his only ploy
And she a by-play. Stupidly he stood
Looking in every flaw of air for her,
And staring close at every bird that rose
Out of the reeds, his shock eyes jumping on
From place to place of her nonentity.
Where had she gone, the hussy? Had she flown
Clean out of time and space? A dream? But no,
For still her nestlings' beaks gaped after her,
And still his nostrils quivered and fanned wide
Like twanged elastic in an ecstasy;
Ear and eye still gonged her striking image.

He called her loudly, then: "Syrinx! Syrinx!"
But nothing blinked: the ignorant ox browsed on,
And the reflective river brassily
Slewed by without a pause. At his foot
Out of the bearded iris rose the bee
In drizzling sibilance. But angrily
Pan stood, and stamped the sudden edge, his hands
Chawed savagely at the sedge. But what, what
Was this they held so closely choked? A reed?
Was ever reed like this one, coolest green,
And blue as if the ice-roots ran in it?
He opened his hands, and looked. O now he knew
The subterfuge of flesh. So this was how
She gave the slip to his lubricity.
He broke into a goat, the Spirit gone:
The Spirit flown, *she* split into a reed:

Green reed, red animal were complements,
And neither could the other venerate.
Her he could feel, but never enter now:
Him she could enter, but could never feel:
So red and green must wrangle endlessly.
Ah, why had he come here? Was it to see
Grass shaken by the wind? Would nothing ease
The nettle-tease of flesh, the salted taws
Of lust?

Grief crowded in his eyes and looked at her,
Till, fogged by too-long thought, he turned away
Lugubriously, lugging the bruised reed:
And with no backward look he went
With bold subtracting steps across the plain
And vanished in the upland groves and haze.
And afterwards was heard
His starving flute crying in stony places,
Calling for love, for love the heavenly rain,
To fall and make his green reed nymph again.
And still he cried 'Syrinx' and still he drew
Her only answer from the reed he blew.

The Swan

Bottomed by tugging combs of water
The slow and loath swan slews and looks
Coldly down through chutes of stilled chatter
Upon the shadows in flight among the stones.

Into abashed confusions of ooze
It dips, and from the muddy fume
The silver and flute-like fishes rise
Endlessly up through all their octaves of gloom

To where the roofed swan suavely swings
Without qualm on the quivering wave
That laves it on, with elbowing wings held wide
Under its eyes' hugged look and architrave.

Jonquil-long its neck adjudicates
Its body's course; aloof and cool
It cons the nonchalant and unseeing air
With its incurious and dispassionate stare.

Slow, slow, it slides, as if not to chafe
The even sleeve of its approach
Stretched stiff and oval in front of it,
Siphoning it on, selfless, silent, and safe.

On that grey lake, frilled round with scufflings
Of foam and milled with muttering,
I saw lingering, late and lightless,
A single swan, swinging, sleek as a sequin.

Negligently bright, wide wings pinned back,
It mooned on the moving water,
And not all the close and gartering dark
Or gathering wind could lift or flatter
That small and dimming image into flight;
Far from shore and free from foresight,
Coiled in its own indifferent mood
It held the heavens, shores, waters and all their brood.

The Net

Quick, woman, in your net
Catch the silver I fling!
O I am deep in your debt,
Draw tight, skin-tight, the string,
And rake the silver in.
No fisher ever yet
Drew such a cunning ring.

Ah, shifty as the fin
Of any fish this flesh
That, shaken to the shin,
Now shoals into your mesh,
Bursting to be held in;
Purse-proud and pebble-hard,
Its pence like shingle showered.

(2 1 3)

Open the haul, and shake
The fill of shillings free,
Let all the satchels break
And leap about the knee
In shoals of ecstasy.
Guineas and gills will flake
At each gull-plunge of me.

Though all the Angels, and
Saint Michael at their head,
Nightly contrive to stand
On guard about your bed,
Yet none dare take a hand,
But each can only spread
His eagle-eye instead.

But I, being man, can kiss
And bed-spread-eagle too;
All flesh shall come to this,
Being less than angel is,
Yet higher far in bliss
As it entwines with you.

Come, make no sound, my sweet;
Turn down the candid lamp
And draw the equal quilt
Over our naked guilt.

THEODORE ROETHKE

Orchids

They lean over the path
Adder-mouthed,
Swaying close to the face,
Coming out, soft and deceptive,

Limp and damp, delicate as a young bird's tongue;
Their fluttery fledgling lips
Move slowly,
Drawing in the warm air.

And at night,
The faint moon falling through whitewashed glass,
The heat going down
So their musky smell comes even stronger,
Drifting down from their mossy cradles:
So many devouring infants!
Soft luminescent fingers,
Lips neither dead nor alive,
Loose ghostly mouths
Breathing.

Dolor

I have known the inexorable sadness of pencils,
Neat in their boxes, dolor of pad and paper-weight,
All the misery of manilla folders and mucilage,
Desolation in immaculate public places,
Lonely reception room, lavatory, switchboard,
The unalterable pathos of basin and pitcher,
Ritual of multigraph, paper-clip, comma,
Endless duplication of lives and objects.
And I have seen dust from the walls of institutions,
Finer than flour, alive, more dangerous than silica,
Sift, almost invisible, through long afternoons of tedium,
Dropping a fine film on nails and delicate eyebrows,
Glazing the pale hair, the duplicate gray standard faces.

Give Way, Ye Gates

1

Believe me, knot of gristle, I bleed like a tree;
I dream of nothing but boards;
I could love a duck.

(2 1 5)

Such music in a skin!
A bird sings in the bush of your bones.
Tufty, the water's loose.
Bring me a finger. This dirt's lonesome for grass.
Are the rats dancing? The cats are.
And you, cat after great milk and vasty fishes,
A moon loosened from a stag's eye,
Twiced me nicely,—
In the green of my sleep,
In the green.

2

Mother of blue and the many changes of hay,
This tail hates a flat path.
I've let my nose out;
I could melt down a stone,—
How is it with the long birds?
May I look too, loved eye?
It's a wink beyond the world.
In the slow rain, who's afraid?
We're king and queen of the right ground.
I'll risk the winter for you.

You tree beginning to know,
You whisper of kidneys,
We'll swinge the instant!—
With jots and jogs and cinders on the floor:
The sea will be there, the great squashy shadows,
Biting themselves perhaps;
The shrillest frogs;
And the ghost of some great howl
Dead in a wall.
In the high-noon of thighs,
In the springtime of stones,
We'll stretch with the great stems.
We'll be at the business of what might be
Looking toward what we are.

3

You child with a beast's heart,
Make me a bird or a bear!
I've played with the fishes
Among the unwrinkling ferns

(2 1 6)

In the wake of a ship of wind;
But now the instant ages,
And my thought hunts another body.
I'm sad with the little owls.

4

Touch and arouse. Suck and sob. Curse and mourn.
It's a cold scrape in a low place.
The dead crow dries on a pole.
Shapes in the shade
Watch.

The mouth asks. The hand takes.
These wings are from the wrong nest.
Who stands in a hole
Never spills.

I hear the clap of an old wind.
The cold knows when to come.
What beats in me
I still bear.

The deep stream remembers:
Once I was a pond.
What slides away
Provides.

The Visitant

1

A cloud moved close. The bulk of the wind shifted.
A tree swayed over water.
A voice said:
Stay. Stay by the slip-ooze. Stay.

Dearest tree, I said, may I rest here?
A ripple made a soft reply.
I waited, alert as a dog.
The leech clinging to a stone waited;
And the crab, the quiet breather.

2

Slow, slow as a fish, she came,
Slow as a fish coming forward,
Swaying in a long wave;
Her skirts not touching a leaf,
Her white arms reaching towards me.

She came without sound,
Without brushing the wet stones,
In the soft dark of early evening,
She came,
The wind in her hair,
The moon beginning.

3

I woke in the first of morning.
Staring at a tree, I felt the pulse of a stone.
Where's she now, I kept saying.
Where's she now, the mountain's downy girl?

But the bright day had no answer.
A wind stirred in a web of appleworms;
The tree, the close willow, swayed.

JEROME ROTHENBERG

The Seventh Hell: of Smoke, where Fire-Raisers
Try in Vain to Escape from a Shower of
Hot Sand Falling from a Cloud . . .

The houses of men are on fire
    Pity the dead in their graves
        And the homes of the living
Pity the roofbeams whose waters burn till they're ash
Pity the old clouds devoured by the clouds of hot sand

And the sweat that's drawn out of metals pity that too
Pity the teeth robbed of gold
            The bones when their skin falls away
Pity man's cry when the sun is born in his cities
And the thunder breaks down his door
                  And pity the rain
For the rain falls on the deserts of man and is lost

If the mind is a house that has fallen
                  Where will the eye find rest
The images rise from the marrow and cry in the blood
Pity man's voice in the smoke-filled days
            And his eyes in the darkness
Pity the sight of his eyes
                     For what can a man see in the darkness
What can he see but the children's bones and the dead sticks
But the places between spaces and the places of sand
And the places of black teeth
                  The faraway places
The black sand carried and the black bones buried
The black veins hanging from the open skin
            And the blood changed to glass in the night
The eye of man is on fire
            A green bird cries from his house
And opens a red eye to death
The sun drops out of a pine tree
                  Brushing the earth with its wings
For what can a man see in the morning
What can he see but the fire-raisers
            The shadow of the fire-raisers lost in the smoke
The shadow of the smoke where the hot sand is falling
The fire-raisers putting a torch to their arms
The green smoke ascending
                  Pity the children of man
Pity their bones when the skin falls away
Pity the skin devoured by fire
            The fire devoured by fire
The mind of man is on fire
            And where will his eye find rest

MURIEL RUKEYSER

The Watchers

FOR CARSON AND REEVES

She said to me, He lay there sleeping
Upon my bed cast down
With all the bitterness dissolved at last,
An innocent peace within a sleeping head;
He could not find his infant war, nor turn
To that particular zoo, his family of the dead.
I saw her smile of power against his deep
Heart, his waking heart,
Her enmity, her sexual dread.

He said to me, She slept and dreaming
Brought round her face
Closer to me in silence than in fire,
But smiled, but smiled, entering her dark life
Whose hours I never knew, wherein she smiles.
Wherein she dim descending breathes upon
My daylight and the color of waking goes.
Deep in his face, the wanderer
Bringing the gifts of legend and the wars,
Conspiracy of opposing images.

In the long room of dream I saw them sleep,
Turned to each other, clear,
With an obliterated look—
Love, god of foreheads, touching then
Their bending foreheads while the voice of sleep
Wept and sang and sang again
In a chanting of fountains,
A chattering of watches,
Love, sang my sleep, the wavelight on the stone.
I weep to go beyond this throne and the waterlight,
To kiss their eyelids for the last time and pass
From the delicate confidence of their sly throats,
The conversation of their flesh of dreams.
And though I weep in my dream,
When I wake I will not weep.

(2 2 0)

Death of a Cat

A sultry, summer evening, the children playing jacks
      in the hot and grimy garage
      under the yellow eyes of their grey cat.
      when the rubbery jack ball
      popped like a bubble into the street
And the cocky cat after its red-streaking path.

Brakes scrunched, the cat shot up like a spark,
      hit harshly over a tilted ear,
      and the cross-legged children screamed
      at the driven death of their pet.
      While I hauled a hose to clean
The clotted pavement stains, I thought of an ancient legend.

In the Irish Golden Age, three fasting clerks on pilgrimage
      sailed hungrily off to sea,
      praying with soft and folded hands
      their serene faith in God's care.
      But the young clerk said in his caution,
"I think I will take the silence of my small, grey cat."

On the rocky shore of an island, they beached the boat
      and kneeled to speak the Psalms;
      the cat crept to a wild wave
      and snatched a salmon from the foam.
      still the clerks doubted the Lord's hand
Until the fish began to burn upon a sudden fire of coals.

Kneeling shadowy on the oily pavement, I saw
      some jelly of the cat's lost brain,
      a little mound of curious cells
      clinging against the asphalt veins
      and fountainhead of lashing water.
Only the hose's full fury washed the cells away.

(221)

The myth of the showering, supernal claw grew old
     in the grey silence of evening.
     lost in the glittering air;
     though as water smashed the cells,
     they flickered in tingling twilight
Like sparks snapping through the foam of a fire.

The Old Peasant Woman at the Monastery of Zagorsk

Her face wrinkles out like tree rings in a cut-off stump;
Dirt lines her muddy, rigid veins.
Sighing, swaying to booming, battering bells,
She hunches on a bench beneath plane trees,
Black kerchief tight around her greying head.
Starlings shoot like darts from golden onion towers;
A throaty choir chants within the cathedral
As the robed priest steps through a screen of ikons,
Long, white beard foaming down his chest.
Through a courtyard, tourists chatter from a bus,
Photographing Muszhiks from some lost grandmother's myth,
Arguing happily, aimlessly, about horse-drawn days;
Their beards, tobacco-stained, bob in the sun
Like buoys marking surface memories over the deep past.
Fluttering at a tourist, the withered face hisses,
"Kam-moon-eest?" "Nyet. Democrat." He shrinks
Away, smiling, from dirt, as she pours over him
With kissing praise, a burning peasant face
In the path of power from Genghis Khan to Stalin.
Back she mutters to hunch on the bench in sun.
Her silent fury of bones hammering the boards.

The Crow-Marble Whores of Paris

Under a new French law, the prostitutes in Paris
cannot solicit. Instead, they stand silently on corners
and in alleys. The birds, the crows, have become statues.

At midnight, sudden, dim-lit isolation
In silent streets, hardening, stiff-legged
Flocks perching on corners, in alleys, doorways,
Beckon with stone arms, peck of crows.
Crow-marble whores: silent caw for customers,
Clutching marble limbs, no memory in shadow-faces,
Dark stance of birds piercing moonlight,
Statues of their carved embraces.

DELMORE SCHWARTZ

Starlight Like Intuition Pierced the Twelve

The starlight's intuitions pierced the twelve,
The brittle night sky sparkled like a tune
Tinkled and tapped out on the xylophone.
Empty and vain, a glittering dune, the moon
Arose too big, and, in the mood which ruled,
Seemed like a useless beauty in a pit;
And then one said, after he carefully spat:
"No matter what we do, he looks at it!

"I cannot see a child or find a girl
Beyond his smile which glows like that spring moon."
"—Nothing no more the same," the second said,
"Though all may be forgiven, never quite healed
The wound I bear as witness, standing by;
No ceremony surely appropriate,
Nor secret love, escape or sleep because
No matter what I do, he looks at it—"

(2 2 3)

"Now," said the third, "no thing will be the same:
I am as one who never shuts his eyes,
The sea and sky no more are marvellous,
And I no longer understand surprise!"
"Now," said the fourth, "nothing will be enough,
—I heard his voice accomplishing all wit:
No word can be unsaid, no deed withdrawn,
—No matter what is said, he measures it!"

"Vision, imagination, hope or dream,
Believed, denied, the scene we wished to see?
It does not matter in the least: for what
Is altered, if it is not true? That we
Saw goodness, as it is—*this* is the awe
And the abyss which we will not forget,
His story now the sky which holds all thought:
No matter what I think, I think of it!"

"And I will never be what once I was,"
Said one for long as narrow as a knife,
"And we will never be what once we were;
We have died once; this is a second life."
"My mind is spilled in moral chaos," one
Righteous as Job exclaimed, "now infinite
Suspicion of my heart stems what I will,
—No matter what I choose, he stares at it!"

"I am as one native in summer places
—Ten weeks' excitement paid for by the rich;
Debauched by that and then all winter bored,"
The sixth declared, "His peak left us a ditch!"
"He came to make this life more difficult,"
The seventh said, "No one will ever fit
His measure's heights, all is inadequate:
No matter what I do, what good is it?"

"He gave forgiveness to us: what a gift!
The eighth chimed in. "But now we know how much
Must be forgiven. But if forgiven, what?
The crime which was will be; and the least touch
Revives the memory: what is forgiveness worth?"

(2 2 4)

The ninth spoke thus: "Who now will ever sit
At ease in Zion at the Easter feast?
No matter what the place, he touches it!"

"And I will always stammer, since he spoke,"
One, who had been most eloquent, said stammering.
"I looked too long at the sun; like too much light,
So too much goodness is a boomerang,"
Laughed the eleventh of the troop. "I must
Try what he tried: I saw the infinite
Who walked the lake and raised the hopeless dead:
No matter what the feat, he first accomplished it!"

So spoke the twelfth; and then the twelve in chorus:
"Unspeakable unnatural goodness is
Risen and shines, and never will ignore us;
He glows forever in all consciousness;
Forgiveness, love, and hope possess the pit,
And bring our endless guilt, like shadow's bars:
No matter what we do, he stares at it!

What pity then deny? what debt defer?
We know he looks at us like all the stars,
And we shall never be as once we were,
This life will never be what once it was!"

WINFIELD TOWNLEY SCOTT

The U.S. Sailor with the Japanese Skull

Bald-bare, bone-bare, and ivory yellow: skull
Carried by a thus two-headed U.S. sailor
Who got it from a Japanese soldier killed
At Guadalcanal in the ever-present war: our

Bluejacket, I mean, aged 20, in August strolled
Among the little bodies on the sand and hunted
Souvenirs: teeth, tags, diaries, boots; but bolder still
Hacked off this head and under a Ginkgo tree skinned it:

(2 2 5)

Peeled with a lifting knife the jaw and cheeks, bared
The nose, ripped off the black-haired scalp and gutted
The dead eyes to these thoughtful hollows: a scarred
But bloodless job, unless it be said brains bleed.

Then, his ship underway, dragged this aft in a net
Many days and nights—the cold bone tumbling
Beneath the foaming wake, weed-worn and salt-cut
Rolling safe among fish and washed with Pacific;

Till on a warm and level-keeled day hauled in
Held to the sun and the sailor, back to a gun-rest,
Scrubbed the cured skull with lye, perfecting this:
Not foreign as he saw it first: death's familiar cast.

Bodiless, fleshless, nameless, it and the sun
Offend each other in strange fascination
As though one of the two were mocked; but nothing is in
This head, or it fills with what another imagines

As: here were love and hate and the will to deal
Death or to kneel before it, death emperor,
Recorded orders without reasons, bomb-blast, still
A child's morning, remembered moonlight on Fujiyama:

All scoured out now by the keeper of this skull
Made elemental, historic, parentless by our
Sailor boy who thinks of home, voyages laden, will
Not say, "Alas! I did not know him at all."

Three American Women and a German Bayonet

Outweighing all, heavy out of the souvenir bundle
The German bayonet: grooved steel socketed in its worn wood
      handle,
Its detached and threatening silence.
Its gun-body lost, the great knife wrested to a personal particu-
      lar violence—

Now bared shamelessly for what it is, here exposed on the
        American kitchen table and circled with the wreath
Of his three women, the hard tool of death.

And while Mary his mother says "I do not like it. Put it down"
Mary the young sister, her eyes gleaming and round,
Giddily giggles as, the awkward toy in her left hand,
She makes impertinent pushes toward his wife who stands
Tolerant of child's play, waiting for her to be done.
His mother says "I wish he had not got it. It is wicked-looking.
        I tell you: Put it down!"
His wife says "All right, Mary: let me have it—it is mine."
Saucily pouting, primly frowning
The sister clangs bayonet on table; walks out
And her mother follows.

Like a live thing in not-to-be trusted stillness,
Like a kind of engine so foreign and self-possessed
As to chill her momently between worship and terror
It lies there waiting alone in the room with her,
Oddly familiar without ever losing strangeness.
Slowly she moves along it a tentative finger
As though to measure and remember its massive, potent length:
Death-deep, tall as life,
For here prized from the enemy, wrenched away captive, his
        dangerous escape and hers.
Mary his wife
Lifts it heavy and wonderful in her hands and with triumphant
        tenderness.

Into the Wind

The child grabbed my hand and made me run with him
Under the slate-dark sky in air chill with grape.

So much November night came rushing toward us
From all four quarters while he danced and sang
As if for a spring morning, and while he ran
A so determined undirected way, I was amazed

(2 2 7)

To hear him ask where we were going, and could only say
Just before I lost him, "Not all the way together."

I heard his diminishing steps and then the wind.

Then the clouds commenced shifting arrangements of light
Of the cold and mensal, unmentionable moon.

ANNE SEXTON

Ringing the Bells

    And this is the way they ring
the bells in Bedlam
and this is the bell-lady
who comes each Tuesday morning
to give us a music lesson
and because the attendants make you go
and because we mind by instinct,
like bees caught in the wrong hive,
we are the circle of the crazy ladies
who sit in the lounge of the mental house
and smile at the smiling woman
who passes us each a bell,
who points at my hand
that holds my bell, E flat,
and this is the gray dress next to me
who grumbles as if it were special
to be old, to be old,
and this is the small hunched squirrel girl
on the other side of me
who picks at the hairs over her lip,
who picks at the hairs over her lip all day,
and this is how the bells really sound,
as untroubled and clean
as a workable kitchen,

and this is always my bell responding
to my hand that responds to the lady
who points at me, E flat;
and although we are no better for it,
they tell you to go. And you do.

The Starry Night

> "That does not keep me from having a terrible need
> of—shall I say the word—religion. Then I go out at
> night to paint the stars."
>   —VINCENT VAN GOGH in a letter to his brother

The town does not exist
except where one black-haired tree slips
up like a drowned woman into the hot sky.
The town is silent. The night boils with eleven stars.
Oh starry starry night! This is how
I want to die.

It moves. They are all alive.
Even the moon bulges in its orange irons
to push children, like a god, from its eye.
The old unseen serpent swallows up the stars.
Oh starry starry night! This is how
I want to die:

into that rushing beast of the night,
sucked up by that great dragon, to split
from my life with no flag,
no belly,
no cry.

The Phenomenon

How lovely it was, after the official fright,
To walk in the shadowy drifts, as if the clouds
Saturated with the obscurity of night
Had died and fallen piecemeal into shrouds.

What crepes there were, what sables heaped on stones,
What soft shakos on posts, tragically gay!
And oil-pool-flooded fields that blackly shone
The more black under the liquid eye of day!

It was almost warmer to the touch than sands
And sweeter-tasting than the white, and yet,
Walking, the children held their fathers' hands
Like visitors to a mine or parapet.

Then black it snowed again and while it fell
You could see the sun, an irritated rim
Wheeling through smoke; each from his shallow hell
Experienced injured vision growing dim.

But one day all was clear, and one day soon,
Sooner than those who witnessed it had died,
Nature herself forgot the phenomenon,
Her faulty snowfall brilliantly denied.

Furnished Lives

I have been walking today
Where the sour children of London's poor sleep
Pressed close to the unfrosted glare
Torment lying close to tenement,
Of the clay fire; I
Have watched their whispering souls flying straight to God:

"O Lord, please give to us
A dinner-service, white, and washed and gay
As a plain of swan-stilled snow;
Lord, flood this room with your outrageous smile."
I have balanced myself on
The needle of the Strand where like a charnel house

Each man and maiden turn
On the deliberate hour of the cock,
As if two new risen souls,
To the cragged landscape of each other's eyes.
But where lover upon lover
Should meet, where sheet, and pillow, and eiderdown

Should frolic and breathe
As dolphins on the stylized crown of the sea
Their pale cerements lie.
They tread with chocolate souls and paper hands,
They walk into that room
Your gay and daffodil smile has never seen:

Not to love's pleasant feast
They go, in the mutations of the night,
But to their humiliations
Paled as a swan's dead feather scorched in the sun.
I have been walking today
Among the newly paper-crowned, among those

Whose casual, paper body
Is crushed between fate's fingers and the platter,
But Sir, their perpetual fire
Was not stubbed out, folded on brass or stone
Extinguished in the dark,
But burns with the drear dampness of cut flowers.

I cannot hear their piped
Cry. These souls have no players. They have resigned
The vivid performance of their world.
And your world, Lord,
Has now become
Like a dumb winter show, held in one room,

Which must now reek of age
Before you have retouched its lips with such straight fire
As through your stony earth
Burns with ferocious tears in the world's eyes;
Church-stone, door-knocker and polished railway lines
Move in their separate dumb way
So why not these lives;
I ask you often, but you never say?

LOUIS SIMPSON

Carentan O Carentan

Trees in the old days used to stand
And shape a shady lane
Where lovers wandered hand in hand
Who came from Carentan.

This was the shining green canal
Where we came two by two
Walking at combat-interval.
Such trees we never knew.

(2 3 2)

The day was early June, the ground
Was soft and bright with dew.
Far away the guns did sound,
But here the sky was blue.

The sky was blue, but there a smoke
Hung still above the sea
Where the ships together spoke
To towns we could not see.

Could you have seen us through a glass
You would have said a walk
Of farmers out to turn the grass,
Each with his own hay-fork.

The watchers in their leopard suits
Waited till it was time,
And aimed between the belt and boot
And let the barrel climb.

I must lie down at once, there is
A hammer at my knee.
And call it death or cowardice,
Don't count again on me.

Everything's alright, Mother,
Everyone gets the same
At one time or another.
It's all in the game.

I never strolled, nor ever shall,
Down such a leafy lane.
I never drank in a canal,
Nor ever shall again.

There is a whistling in the leaves
And it is not the wind,
The twigs are falling from the knives
That cut men to the ground.

(2 3 3)

Tell me, Master-Sergeant,
The way to turn and shoot.
But the Sergeant's silent
That taught me how to do it.

O Captain, show us quickly
Our place upon the map.
But the Captain's sickly
And taking a long nap.

Lieutenant, what's my duty,
My place in the platoon?
He too's a sleeping beauty,
Charmed by that strange tune.

Carentan O Carentan
Before we met with you
We never yet had lost a man
Or known what death could do.

A Story about Chicken Soup

In my grandmother's house there was always chicken soup
And talk of the old country—mud and boards,
Poverty,
The snow falling down the necks of lovers.

Now and then, out of her savings
She sent them a dowry. Imagine
The rice-powdered faces!
And the smell of the bride, like chicken soup.

But the Germans killed them.
I know it's in bad taste to say it,
But it's true. The Germans killed them all.

*

In the ruins of Berchtesgaden
A child with yellow hair
Ran out of a doorway.

A German girl-child—
Cuckoo, all skin and bones—
Not even enough to make chicken soup.
She sat by the stream and smiled.

Then as we splashed in the sun
She laughed at us.
We had killed her mechanical brothers,
So we forgave her.

*

The sun is shining.
The shadows of the lovers have disappeared.
They are all eyes; they have some demand on me—
They want me to be more serious than I want to be.

They want me to stick in their mudhole
Where no one is elegant.
They want me to wear old clothes,
They want me to be poor, to sleep in a room with many others—

Not to walk in the painted sunshine
To a summer house,
But to live in the tragic world forever.

ROBIN   SKELTON

"Angel"

They called her "Angel," sardonic
at bitter scrubbing arm
sharp as a scraped white shinbone
there in the chicken run
for hens to clack at, mottled
brown by the rain and sun.

(2 3 5)

She was the sour-faced snatcher
at every gossip's tale,
bent graceless, thankless, angular,
over the clanging pail,
the wet wood rough with scrubbing,
the hot carbolic smell.

Yes, she was bitter, God knows—
bitter and sour and quick
to vex as a thistle blurting
its milk at a swung stick;
her head was a mortification
of curlers and twisted grips.

So "Angel" they called her, laughing.
Her son was a big lad,
simple and shy and clumsy.
If ever she had a glad
softness for him she kept it dark,
abused all the luck she had.

And died. But before that last
vengeful retort to breath
she saw him wed and settled.
"Poor Angel" they said at his wreath.
And the women removed the tight curlers
once she lay small in death.

The Brigg

It was six foot four of my father
balanced upon the jag
of the green-brown rock with his bright rod
after the long drag
round from the bay over weed-raked pools
that made me see the Brigg.

His hair was white as the flying spume,
his hand as hard as wood,
his eyes blue as the blue pool
that mirrored how he stood,
holding within its depthless rock
sky-space, man, and flood.

(2 3 6)

Inverted there like a totem hung
down into the sky
where spectral gulls involved the weed
with gaping soundless cry,
he fished a far unbeing sea
no man might profit by.

I watched him, back towards the pool,
cast out into the foam
beyond the ledge of rock on rock;
I watched him stand alone,
one man as tall as any tower,
and one deep as stone.

A. J. M. SMITH

Business as Usual 1946

Across the craggy indigo
Come rumours of the flashing spears,
And in the clank of rancid noon
There is a tone, and such a tone.

How tender! How insidious!
The air grows gentle with protecting bosks,
And furry leaves take branch and root.
Here we are safe, we say, and slyly smile.

In this delightful forest, fluted so,
We burghers of the sunny central plain
Fable a still refuge from the spears
That clank—but gently clank—but clank again!

What Is That Music High in the Air?

A voice from the heroic dead,
Unfaltering and clear,
Rings from the overhead
And zips into the ear;

But what it was it said
Or what it meant to say,
This clarion of the sacred dead,
I cannot tell today;

And tomorrow will be late,
For the ear shall turn to clay
And the scrannel pipe will grate,
Shiver, and die away,

A sigh of the inconsequential dead,
A murmur in a drain,
Lapping a severed head,
Unlaurelled, unlamented, vain.

Brigadier

A Song of French Canada

One Sunday morning soft and fine
Two old campaigners let their nags meander;
One was a Sergeant of the Line,
The other a Brigade Commander.
The General spoke with martial roar,
'Nice weather for this time of year!'
  And 'Right you are,' replied Pandore,
  'Right you are, my Brigadier.'

'A Guardsman's is a thankless calling,
Protecting private property,
In summer or when snows are falling,
From malice, rape, or robbery;

(2 3 8)

While the wife whom I adore
Sleeps alone and knows no cheer.'
  And 'Right you are,' replied Pandore,
  'Right you are, my Brigadier.'

'I have gathered Glory's laurel
With the rose of Venus twined—
I am Married, and a General;
Yet, by Jesus, I've a mind
To start like Jason for the golden shore
And follow my Star—away from here!'
  'Ah, right you are,' replied Pandore,
  'Right you are, my Brigadier.'

'I remember the good days of my youth
And the old songs that rang
So cheerily. In that time, forsooth,
I had a doting mistress, full of tang . . .
But, ah! the heart—I know not wherefore—
Loves to change its bill of fare.'
  And 'Right you are,' replied Pandore,
  'Right you are, my Brigadier.'

Now Phoebus neared his journey's end;
Our heroes' shadows fell behind:
Yet still the Sergeant did attend,
And still the General spoke his mind.
'Observe,' he said, 'how more and more
Yon orb ensanguines all the sphere.'
  And 'Right you are,' replied Pandore,
  'Right you are, my Brigadier.'

They rode in silence for a while:
You only heard the measured tread
Of muffled hoof beats, mile on mile—
But when Aurora, rosy red,
Unbarred her Eastern door,
The faint refrain still charmed the ear,
  As 'Right you are,' replied Pandore,
  'Right you are, my Brigadier.'

FROM *Heart's Needle*

6

    Easter has come around
again; the river is rising
    over the thawed ground
and the banksides. When you come you bring
    an egg dyed lavender.
We shout along our bank to hear
our voices returning from the hills to meet us.
    We need the landscape to repeat us.

    You lived on this bank first.
While nine months filled your term, we knew
    how your lungs, immersed
in the womb, miraculously grew
    their useless folds till
the fierce, cold air rushed in to fill
them out like bushes thick with leaves. You took your hour,
    caught breath, and cried with your full lung power.

    Over the stagnant bight
we see the hungry bank swallow
    flaunting his free flight
still; we sink in mud to follow
    the killdeer from the grass
that hides her nest. That March there was
rain; the rivers rose; you could hear killdeers flying
    all night over the mudflats crying.

    You bring back how the red-
winged blackbird shrieked, slapping frail wings,
    diving at my head—
I saw where her tough nest, cradled, swings
    in tall reeds that must sway
with the winds blowing every way.
If you recall much, you recall this place. You still
    live nearby—on the opposite hill.

After the sharp windstorm
of July Fourth, all that summer
    through the gentle, warm
afternoons, we heard great chain saws chirr
    like iron locusts. Crews
of roughneck boys swarmed to cut loose
branches wrenched in the shattering wind, to hack free
    all the torn limbs that could sap the tree.

    In the debris lay
starlings, dead. Near the park's birdrun
    we surprised one day
a proud, tan-spatted, buff-brown pigeon.
    In my hands she flapped so
fearfully that I let her go.
Her keeper came. And we helped snarl her in a net.
    You bring things I'd as soon forget.

    You raise into my head
a Fall night that I came once more
    to sit on your bed;
sweat beads stood out on your arms and fore-
    head and you wheezed for breath,
for help, like some child caught beneath
its comfortable woolly blankets, drowning there.
    Your lungs caught and would not take the air.

    Of all things, only we
have power to choose that we should die;
    nothing else is free
in this world to refuse it. Yet I,
    who say this, could not raise
myself from bed how many days
to the thieving world. Child, I have another wife,
    another child. We try to choose our life.

7

Here in the scuffled dust
    is our ground of play.
I lift you on your swing and must
    shove you away,

(241)

see you return again,
    drive you off again, then

stand quiet till you come.
    You, though you climb
higher, farther from me, longer,
    will fall back to me stronger.
Bad penny, pendulum,
    you keep my constant time

to bob in blue July
    where fat goldfinches fly
over the glittering, fecund
    reach of our growing lands.
Once more now, this second,
    I hold you in my hands.

GARY SNYDER

FROM *Logging*

3

"Lodgepole Pine: the wonderful reproductive
power of this species on areas over which its
stand has been killed by fire is dependent upon
the ability of the closed cones to endure a fire
which kills the tree without injuring its seed.
After fire, the cones open and shed their seeds
on the bared ground and a new growth springs
up."

Stood straight
                holding the choker high
As the Cat swung back the arch
                piss-firs falling,

Limbs snapping on the tin hat
                    bright D caught on
Swinging butt-hooks
                    ringing against cold steel.
Hsü Fang lived on leeks and pumpkins.
Goosefoot,
            wild herbs,
                        fields lying fallow!

But it's hard to farm
Between the stumps:
The cows get thin, the milk tastes funny,
The kids grow up and go to college
They don't come back.
                    the little fir-trees do.

            Rocks the same blue as sky
Only icefields, a mile up,
                        are the mountain
Hovering over ten thousand acres
Of young fir.

8

Each dawn is clear
Cold air bites the throat.
Thick frost on the pine bough
Leaps from the tree
            snapped by the diesel

Drifts and glitters in the
                    horizontal sun.
In the frozen grass
            smoking boulders
            ground by steel tracks.
In the frozen grass
            wild horses stand
            beyond a row of pines.
The D8 tears through piss-fir,
Scrapes the seed-pine
                    chipmunks flee,
A black ant carries an egg
Aimlessly from the battered ground.
Yellowjackets swarm and circle

Above the crushed dead-log, their home.
Pitch oozes from barked
       trees still standing,
Mashed bushes make strange smells.
Lodgepole pines are brittle.
Camprobbers flutter to watch.

A few stumps, drying piles of brush;
Under the thin duff, a toe-scrape down
Black lava of a late flow.
Leaves stripped from thornapple
Taurus by nightfall.

The Late Snow and Lumber Strike of the Summer of Fifty-four

Whole towns shut down
       hitching the Coast road, only gypos
Running their beat trucks, no logs on
Gave me rides. Loggers all gone fishing
Chainsaws in a pool of cold oil
On back porches of ten thousand
Split-shake houses, quiet in summer rain.
Hitched north all of Washington
Crossing and re-crossing the passes
Blown like dust, no place to work.

Climbing the steep ridge below Shuksan
       clumps of pine
       float out the fog
No place to think or work
       drifting.

On Mt. Baker, alone
In a gully of blazing snow:
Cities down the long valleys west
Thinking of work, but here,
Burning in sun-glare
Below a wet cliff, above a frozen lake,

The whole Northwest on strike
Black burners cold,
The green-chain still,
I must turn and go back:
        caught on a snowpeak
        between heaven and earth
And stand in lines in Seattle.
Looking for work.

WILLIAM STAFFORD

Traveling Through the Dark

Traveling through the dark I found a deer
dead on the edge of the Wilson River road.
It is usually best to roll them into the canyon:
that road is narrow; to swerve might make more dead.

By glow of the tail-light I stumbled back of the car
and stood by the heap, a doe, a recent killing;
she had stiffened already, almost cold.
I dragged her off: she was large in the belly.

My fingers touching her side brought me the reason—
her side was warm; her fawn lay there waiting,
alive, still, never to be born.
Beside that mountain road I hesitated.

The car aimed ahead its lowered parking lights;
under the hood purred the steady engine.
I stood in the glare of the warm exhaust turning red;
around our group I could hear the wilderness listen.

I thought hard for us all—my only swerving—,
then pushed her over the edge into the river.

Cora Punctuated with Strawberries

Sandra and that boy that's going to get her in trouble
one of these days were out in the garden where anyone in
Mother's sickroom could see them out the upperleft corner of the
window sitting behind the garage feeding each other
blueberries and Cherry was helping with the dishes alone in the
kitchen and
um good strawberries if we did grow them just can't can without
popping one in every so often Henry was at it again in the
attic with that whatchamacallit of his when the Big
Bomb fell smack in the MacDonalds' yard you know over on
Elm and they got into Life and the papers and all all very
well but they might have been in when it hit and it would have
been a very different story for Lucy MacDonald then I'll tell
you well they say it was right in the Geographic Center of the
country the Geographic
woody Center you could hear it just as plain I thought the
elevator had blown up and I guess you read yourself the awful
things it would have
ak another one woody I tell you I don't know what's got
into these strawberries used to be so juicy they
say they only had the one and it's all it would have took well I
always knew we could beat the enemy they made such
shoddy tricks and spring-toys and puzzles and fuses and
things and besides, it wouldn't have been right.

News from the Cabin

1

Hairy was here.
He hung on a sumac seed pod.
Part of his double tail hugged the crimson
    scrotum under cockscomb leaves—
    or call it blushing lobster claw, that swatch—
    a toothy match to Hairy's red skullpatch.
Cried *peek!* Beaked it—chiselled the drupe.
His nostril I saw, slit in a slate whistle.
White-black dominoes clicked in his wings.
Bunched beneath the dangle he heckled with holes,
    bellysack soft, eye a brad, a red-flecked
    mallet his ball-peen head, his neck its haft.

2

Scurry was here.
He sat up like a six-inch bear,
    rocked on the porch with me;
    brought his own chair, his chow-haired tail.
Ate a cherry I threw.
Furry paunch, birchbark-snowy, pinecone-brown back,
    a jacket with sleeves to the digits.
Sat put, pert, neat, in his suit and his seat, for a minute,
    a frown between snub ears, bulb-eyed head
    toward me sideways, chewed.
Rocked, squeaked. Stored the stone in his cheek.
Finished, fell to all fours, a little roan couch;
    flurried paws loped him off, prone-bodied,
    tail turned torch, sail, scarf.

3

Then, Slicker was here.
Dipped down, cobalt and turquoise brushes
    fresh as paint. Gripped a pine-tassle,

folded his flaunts, parted his pointed nib, and scrawled
  jeeah! on the air.
Japanned so smooth, his head-peak and all his shaft:
  harsh taunts from that dovey shape, soft tints—
  nape and chin black-splintered, quilltips white-lashed.
Javelin-bird, he slurred his color,
  left his ink-bold word here; flashed off.
Morning prints his corvine noise elsewhere,
  while that green toss still quivers with his equipoise.

4

And Supple was here.
Lives nearby at the stump.
Trickled out from under, when the sun struck there.
Mud-and-silver-licked, his length—a single spastic muscle—
  slid over stones and twigs to a snuggle of roots, and hid.
I followed that elastic: loose
  unicolored knot, a noose he made as if unconscious.
Until my shadow touched him: half his curd
  shuddered, the rest lay chill.
I stirred: the ribbon raised a loop;
  its end stretched, then cringed like an udder;
  a bifid tongue, his only rapid, whirred
  in the vent; vertical pupils lit his hood.
That part, a groping finger, hinged, stayed upright.
Indicated what? That I stood
  in his light? I left the spot.

R. S. THOMAS

Too Late

I would have spared you this, Prytherch;
You were like a child to me.
I would have seen you poor and in rags,
Rather than wealthy and not free.

The rain and wind are hard masters;
I have known you wince under their lash.
But there was comfort for you at the day's end
Dreaming over the warm ash

Of a turf fire on a hill farm,
Contented with your accustomed ration
Of bread and bacon, and drawing your strength
From membership of an old nation

Not given to beg. But look at yourself
Now, a servant hired to flog
The life out of the slow soil,
Or come obediently as a dog

To the pound's whistle. Can't you see
Behind the smile on the times' face
The cold face of the machine
That will destroy you and your race?

Welcome

You can come in.
You can come a long way;
We can't stop you.
You can come up the roads
Or by railway;
You can land from the air.
You can walk this country
From end to end;
But you won't be inside;
You must stop at the bar,
The old bar of speech.

We have learnt your own
Language, but don't
Let it take you in;
It's not what you mean,
It's what you pay with
Everywhere you go,

Pleased at the price
In shop windows.
There is no way there;
Past town and factory
You must travel back
To the cold bud of water
In the hard rock.

Strangers

We don't like your white cottage.
We don't like the way you live.
Their sins are venial, the folk
With green blouses you displace.
They have gone proudly away,
Leaving only the dry bed
Of footsteps where there was grass,
Or memory of a face
For ever setting within the glass
Of windows about the door.

You have not been here before.
You will offend with your speech
Winds that preferred hands
Wrung with despair, profound
Audiences of the dead.

ANTHONY THWAITE

Manhood End

At Manhood End the older dead lie thick
Together by the churchyard's eastern wall.
The sexton sweated out with spade and pick
And moved turf, clay, bones, gravestones, to make room
For later comers, those whose burial
Was still far off, but who would need a tomb.

Among the pebbles, in the molehills' loam,
Turned thighbone up, and skull: whatever frail
Relic was left was given a new home,
Close to the wood and farther from the sea.
Couch-grass grew stronger here and, with the pale
Toadstools and puffballs, masked that vacancy.

In April, on a day when rain and sun
Had stripped all distances to clarity,
I stood there by the chapel, and saw one
Lean heron rising on enormous wings
Across the silted harbour towards the sea.
Dead flowers at my feet: but no one brings

Flowers to those shifted bodies. The thin flies,
First flies of spring, stirred by the rain-butt. Names
Stared at me out of moss, the legacies
Of parents to their children: *Lucy, Ann,*
Names I have given, which a father claims
Because they mean something that he began.

Cool in the chapel of St. Wilfred, I
Knelt by the Saxon wall and bowed my head,
Shutting my eyes: till, looking up to high
Above the pews, I saw a monument,
A sixteenth-century carving, with the dead
Husband and wife kneeling together, meant

For piety and remembrance. But on their right
I grasped with sudden shock a scene less pure—
A naked woman, arms bound back and tight,
And breasts thrust forward to be gnawed by great
Pincers two men held out. I left, unsure
Of what that emblem meant; and towards the gate

The small mounds of the overcrowded dead
Shrank in the sun. The eastern wall seemed built
Of darker stone. I lay: and by my head
A starling with its neck snapped; nestling there,
A thrush's egg with yolk and white half split,
And one chafed bone a molehill had laid bare.

(2 5 1)

Frail pictures of the world at Manhood End—
How we are shifted, smashed, how stones display
The names and passions that we cannot mend.
The lych-gate stood and showed me, and I felt
The pebbles teach my feet. I walked away,
My head full of the smell my nostrils smelt.

CHARLES TOMLINSON

Paring the Apple

There are portraits and still-lifes.

And there is paring the apple.

And then? Paring it slowly,
From under cool-yellow
Cold-white emerging. And . . . ?

The spring of concentric peel
Unwinding off white,
The blade hidden, dividing.

There are portraits and still-lifes
And the first, because "human"
Does not excel the second, and
Neither is less weighted
With a human gesture, than paring the apple
With a human stillness.

The cool blade
Severs between coolness, apple-rind
Compelling a recognition.

Farewell to Van Gogh

The quiet deepens. You will not persuade
  One leaf of the accomplished, steady, darkening
Chestnut-tower to displace itself
  With more of violence than the air supplies
When, gathering dusk, the pond brims evenly
  And we must be content with stillness.

Unhastening, daylight withdraws from us its shapes
  Into their central calm. Stone by stone
Your rhetoric is dispersed until the earth
  Becomes once more the earth, the leaves
A sharp partition against cooling blue.

Farewell, and for your instructive frenzy
  Gratitude. The world does not end tonight
And the fruit that we shall pick tomorrow
  Await us, weighing the unstripped bough.

The Cavern

Obliterate
mythology as you unwind
this mountain-interior
into the negative-dark mind,
as there
the gypsum's snow
the limestone stair
and boneyard landscape grow
into the identity of flesh.

Pulse of the water-drop,
veils and scales, fins
and flakes of the forming
leprous rock,
how should these
inhuman, turn
human with such chill affinities.

(2 5 3)

Hard to the hand,
these mosses not of moss,
but nostrils, pits
of eyes, faces
in flight and prints
of feet where no feet ever were,
elude the mind's
hollow that would contain
this canyon within a mountain.

Not far
enough from the familiar,
press
in under a deeper dark until
the curtained sex
the arch, the streaming buttress
have become
the self's unnameable and shaping home.

JOHN WAIN

Poem without a Main Verb

Watching oneself
being clever, being clever:
keeping the keen equipoise between *always* and *never*;

delicately divining
(the gambler's sick art)
which of the strands must hold, and which may part;

playing off, playing off
with pointless cunning
the risk of remaining against the risk of running;

(2 5 4)

balancing, balancing
(alert and knowing)
the carelessly hidden with the carefully left showing;

endlessly, endlessly
finely elaborating
the filigree threads in the web and the bars in the grating;

at last minutely
and thoroughly lost
in the delta where profit fans into cost;

with superb navigation
afloat on that darkening, deepening sea,
helplessly, helplessly.

Anecdote of 2 A.M.

"Why was she lost?" my darling said aloud
With never a movement in her sleep. I lay
Awake and watched her breathe, remote and proud.

Her words reached out where I could never be.
She dreamed a world remote from all I was.
"Why was she lost?" She was not asking me.

I knew that there was nothing I could say.
She breathed and dreamed beyond our kisses' sphere.
My watchful night was her unconscious day.

I could not tell what dreams disturbed her heart.
She spoke, and never knew my tongue was tied.
I longed to bless her but she lay apart.

That was our last night, if I could have known.
But I remember still how in the dark
She dreamed her question and we lay alone.

On an Italian Hillside

On a hillside in Italy
The air shook like a single grass
In a secret morning wind
That moves no other about it,
And moves it only,
Awaiting the waiting thoughts and themes of the day.

From a hillside in Italy
The sea was a child's blue slate
With toy craft signing their furrows
In chalk-marks, moved
By no child's hand, appearing,
Scratching in silence the tilted slate of the sea.

Above a hillside in Italy
The sun sank like a paper rose
Through water, dyeing it red,
Or like a drop of scarlet
Water-colour falling and softening
Into the yellow on already wet water-colour paper.

Below a hillside in Italy
The darkness filled the bay
Like flood-water, pushing
Down all opposition, submerging
The ships, the olive trees, the town,
The little gripping houses, the slipping rocks.

On a hillside in Italy
The lights came out like stars, steadied
In the net of haze over the sea,
And night climbed the hill to the top
To sit watching the twinkling fishboats
On the secret, slate-dark, flowering, flooded sea.

O'Reilly's Reply

Let's say I live here, at any rate,
In the carefully careless country of England,
Where the humans are countless as a drift of sand,
Where John Betjeman shares in the trying confusions
Of young men who can sell their angry allusions
To the illusion of living in the Wellfed State.

Let's say I lose here, in a sense,
The sense of a freedom to live and die.
Where I come from, they either fight or multiply.
Here, in a country which once had charm,
The peasant walks in tweeds and does no one harm
And talks without a trace of innocence.

Let's say I love here, in a way,
Where the poet perfecting his poems before dark
May pick his writing-paper from the litter in the park.
Perhaps the place is like a hundred other places
Where a traffic-light only can stop the flow of faces.
Perhaps it's unlikely, but I'd like to stay.

THEODORE WEISS

Preface

"Sonja Henie," the young girl,
looking out of the evening paper,
cries, "just got married!"

"I don't care if she did,"
the mother replies. "She's been
married before; it's nothing new."

(2 5 7)

Darnel, Ragweed, Wortle

and turning to me, the young poet
tries to say once more what weeds
mean to him—
            luscious weeds
riding high, wholly personal:
"O go ahead, hack away as much
as you like; I've been thrown out
of better places than this"—

his face just come back from staring
out the window into a day
wandering somewhere in early fall
and a long quiet contented rain,

the sky still on his face, the barn
out there, green-roofed and shiny,
gay in a wet way with its red
wet-streaked sides.
            I read his poem,
mainly about how much it likes weeds,
how definite they are, yet how hard
to come by.
            I say, "Like all the rest
only their own face will do, each
a star squinting through 30,000 years
of storm for its particular sky."
And as though a dream should try
to recollect its dreamer, we look out
across the long highways of rain,
look out

Darnel, Ragweed, Wortle

I do not say what we both are thinking
as we see it flicker in that rain-
soaked day: the face exceeding
face, name, and memory,
yet clinging to our thoughts.
            Black
against the sky, a flock of cranes
shimmers, one unbroken prickly rhythm,

wave on wave, keeping summer jaunty
in its midst.
                    And Sonja Henie,
the star, the thin-ice skater,
after many tries, tries once more.

"The poem's not right. I know,
though I worked at it again and again,
I didn't get those old weeds through.
I'm not satisfied, but I'm not done
                    with it yet."

        There in that wheatfield
    of failures, beside all manner
of barns, frost already experimenting,
        the slant of weather definitely
            fall, lovely scratchy

        Darnel, Ragweed, Wortle

The Reapings

    The firstlings of grief,
    pain in all its sweetest fat
    and dew, abounding in my sinews
    its sinews, like a mettlesome, gay
    youth . . .
                    years later,
    the fields gone over a thousand
    times, every flower spied on,
    every weed, like a royal being,
    golden foreigner,
                    as though
    one, not seeing, might forget,
    let loose its secret, the reality . . .
    years later, the basic truths,
    their seasons

in each season,
gone over and over, still grief
strikes, a new-forged arrow, finds
out fresh wounds, sly resources,
surprising, terrible,
                         of pain.
The hands clutch themselves
in the wrestle; how learn
to let go like a nakedness in this
fluent fall,
                 a warbling rain?
And how be thankful, name
with love this one that seeks
me out, demands a stature of me,
a strength,
                 so arrogant for me,
I hardly knew I own? I, breaking,
lie there, threshed, before me,
the gifts, the firstlings, weathered
on that forging stone.

In the Round

Catching yourself, hands lathery
and face ajar, inside the glass,
you wryly smile; watching, you know
you're in for it:
                     there in the twinkle
of your eye the horny butting goat
and jutting horny bull, the weasel,
goose bedraggled and the wren
with greedy bill go flashing by;
there too, recoiled as from the shadow
of itself in a teetering pool, claws
contracted to one cry, the spider
crouches in its den.
                         What gusto
this that blows its violence

through a locust's violin, mad summer
burnishing in such midge mouths?

These the routine heroes, poised,
in resolution black as bulls,
deadlocked in a din of warriors
grappling centaurs—prizes near:
a heifer nibbling grass; the rouged
and gossamer girl, nothing diaphanous
as the fearful hope that flits,
a fire's touch, inside her breath,
each prize forgotten—on a vase.

One wonders how the clay withstands
not only time, but what such hands,
great hearts, command from one another,
art and earth, the audience amazed.

Still, though clay crack, necks
break, twitchy as a cock, they stand,
engrossed and going on, a Bach
of a beetle, strutting like a yokel,
nightlong at its tongs and bones.

REED WHITTEMORE

On the Suicide of a Friend

Some there are who are present at such occasions,
And conduct themselves with appropriate feeling and grace.
But they are the rare ones. Mostly the friends and relations
Are caught playing cards or eating miles from the place.
What happens on that dark river, or road, or mountain
Passes unnoticed as friend trumps loved one's ace.

Perhaps he knew this about them—worse, he did not,
And raged over the brink of that road or mountain
Thinking at least they'd remember before they forgot.
Either way, now he is dead and done with that lot.

The Self and the Weather

It is tiresome always to talk about weather, or think about it.
We ought to be able to rise (always rise) above it
By dedication
To our jobs, wives, children, even our art. Thus this poem,
If it is a poem,
Ought (always ought)
Not to be written.
If I must lie
On this rumpled bed with my clipboard and pencil
And moodily stare out windows at wet leaves,
Wet grass, wet laundry and so on, hearing the thunder
Rattle, and thinking that last night the weatherman said that
Today (!) (irony)
Would be a *marvelous* day—if, as I say,
I must lie here and weakly succumb to such outdoor trivia,
Then the least that I or anyone trapped with a clipboard
Should (always should) do
Is not this.
                    True.

This is always true.
It was true some time ago when Antony ditched
The Egyptian fleet—a girl was the weather
That day—and true too when Macbeth found somebody
Sitting where he was to sit (but the chair was empty).
Indeed one could dazzle the world with instances, mostly
From Shakespeare, proving
That any man of resolve, any man with a mission
Should not
Do what he does but should rise (always rise)
To where it is sunny; and there, undistracted
By anything but a hurricane, say, or a change

Of administration, should keep
Close to his clipboard and write, if he writes,
Treatises mostly, not poems, for treatises seldom
Traffic in weather as poems do,
And may (the treatises) best be composed in a windowless
Room underground where the outside world
Is represented ideally by four white walls
And a picture by some gay cubist of what could not possibly
Be wet leaves, wet grass, wet laundry, and so on.

RICHARD   WILBUR

The Death of a Toad

A toad the power mower caught,
Chewed and clipped of a leg, with a hobbling hop has got
    To the garden verge, and sanctuaried him
    Under the cineraria leaves, in the shade
        Of the ashen heartshaped leaves, in a dim,
            Low, and a final glade.

The rare original heartsblood goes,
Spends on the earthen hide, in the folds and wizenings, flows
    In the gutters of the banked and staring eyes. He lies
    As still as if he would return to stone,
        And soundlessly attending, dies
            Toward some deep monotone,

Toward misted and ebullient seas
And cooling shores, toward lost Amphibia's emperies.
    Day dwindles, drowning, and at length is gone
    In the wide and antique eyes, which still appear
        To watch, across the castrate lawn,
            The haggard daylight steer.

Marginalia

Things concentrate at the edges; the pond-surface
Is bourne to fish and man and it is spread
In textile scum and damask light, on which
The lily-pads are set; and there are also
    Inlaid ruddy twigs, becalmed pine-leaves,
    Air-baubles, and the chain mail of froth.

Descending into sleep (as when the night-lift
Falls past a brilliant floor), we glimpse a sublime
Décor and hear, perhaps, a complete music,
But this evades us, as in the night meadows
    The crickets' million roundsong dies away
    From all advances, rising in every distance.

Our riches are centrifugal; men compose
Daily, unwittingly, their final dreams,
And those are our own voices whose remote
Consummate chorus rides on the whirlpool's rim,
    Past which we flog our sails, toward which we drift,
    Plying our trades, in hopes of a good drowning.

Advice to a Prophet

When you come, as you soon must, to the streets of our city,
Mad-eyed from stating the obvious,
Not proclaiming our fall but begging us
In God's name to have self-pity,

Spare us all word of the weapons, their force and range,
The long numbers that rocket the mind;
Our slow, unreckoning hearts will be left behind,
Unable to fear what is too strange.

Nor shall you scare us with talk of the death of the race.
How should we dream of this place without us?—
The sun mere fire, the leaves untroubled about us,
A stone look on the stone's face?

(2 6 4)

Speak of the world's own change. Though we cannot conceive
Of an undreamt thing, we know to our cost
How the dreamt cloud crumbles, the vines are blackened by
                frost,
How the view alters. We could believe,

If you told us so, that the white-tailed deer will slip
Into perfect shade, grown perfectly shy,
The lark avoid the reaches of our eye,
The jack-pine lose its knuckled grip

On the cold ledge, and every torrent burn
As Xanthus once, its gliding trout
Stunned in a twinkling. What should we be without
The dolphin's arc, the dove's return,

These things in which we have seen ourselves and spoken?
Ask us, prophet, how we shall call
Our natures forth when that live tongue is all
Dispelled, that glass obscured or broken

In which we have said the rose of our love and the clean
Horse of our courage, in which beheld
The singing locust of the soul unshelled,
And all we mean or wish to mean.

Ask us, ask us whether with the worldless rose
Our hearts shall fail us; come demanding
Whether there shall be lofty or long standing
When the bronze annals of the oak-tree close.

An Invocation to the Goddess

O sea born and obscene
Venus I see ascend
Fishbright upon a shell
Out of a salty pool
Angels and flesh attend,
The dolphin-sewn and blown
Mirrors of sea surround
As bawdy as a boy
That blank desirous form.
The goddess smiles from joy,
I look her in the groin;
Her seakale coloured eyes
Acknowledge her concern.
Not the ideal but real
Half sheltered by her hand,
Sty of ambiguities
Offensive and divine.
Venus preferring joy
Defenceless from the sea
Attending to defend,
Feminine, debonair,
Step naked to the shore.
Step, wound in your hair,
And singing galleries
Fish, fowl, flesh, surround you.
I cry your worshipper
Upon this island ground
Down by a sky and still
Crying borne by a sea,
Rejected and acclaimed.
Announce perfection, smile
Upon what is deformed,
Accept what is, and be.
Beach, beach your scallop here

By pillars of a sea
Whose black-backed dolphins plunge,
Plunge and thrash salty hair.

JAMES WRIGHT

Saint Judas

When I went out to kill myself, I caught
A pack of hoodlums beating up a man.
Running to spare his suffering, I forgot
My name, my number, how my day began,
How soldiers milled around the garden stone
And sang amusing songs; how all that day
Their javelins measured crowds; how I alone
Bargained the proper coins, and slipped away.

Banished from heaven, I found this victim beaten,
Stripped, kneed, and left to cry. Dropping my rope
Aside, I ran, ignored the uniforms:
Then I remembered bread my flesh had eaten,
The kiss that ate my flesh. Flayed without hope,
I held the man for nothing in my arms.

Eisenhower's Visit to Franco, 1959

". . . we die of cold, and not of darkness."
—UNAMUNO

The American hero must triumph over
The forces of darkness.
He has flown through the very light of heaven
And come down in the slow dusk
Of Spain.

(2 6 7)

Franco stands in a shining circle of police.
His arms open in welcome.
He promises all dark things
Will be hunted down.

State police yawn in the prisons.
Antonio Machado follows the moon
Down a road of white dust,
To a cave of silent children
Under the Pyrenees.
Wine darkens in stone jars in villages.
Wine sleeps in the mouths of old men, it is dark red color.

Smiles glitter in Madrid.
Eisenhower has touched hands with Franco, embracing
In a glare of photographers.
Clean new bombers from America muffle their engines
And glide down now.

MARYA ZATURENSKA

Song

Life with her weary eyes,
Smiles, and lifts high her horn
Of plenty and surprise,
Not so where I was born

In the dark streets of fear,
In the damp houses where greed
Grew sharper every year
Through hunger and through need.

Lest the harsh atmosphere
Corrode, defeat, destroy
I built a world too clear,
Too luminous for joy.

Unnatural day on night
I built—tall tower on tower,
Bright on supernal light
Transfixed the too-bright flower.

But see how it has grown!
The cold dream melts, the frost
Dissolves,—the dream has sown
A harvest never lost.

Blood runs into the veins,
The wild hair in the wind
Waves in the natural rains;
The harsh world and unkind

Smiles, and its eye grown mild
Surveys this nothingness
Like an indifferent child
Too sleepy to undress.

Notes on the Poets

The following notes on the poets represented in this anthology are intended to provide only a minimal identification of them and a highly selective list of their books of poems.

DANNIE ABSE, *Welsh,* b. 1923. London physician; playwright, anthologist, leader of "Maverick" group, journalist (medical correspondent). *Tenants of the House,* 1957; *Poems Golders Green,* 1962.

A. ALVAREZ, *English,* b. 1929. Critic, journalist, poetry editor of *The Observer;* occasional visiting professor. Outstanding English advocate of "extremist" confessional poetry after the manner of Robert Lowell, as opposed to the "Movement" poetry represented in the anthologies of Robert Conquest.

KINGSLEY AMIS, *English,* b. 1922. University teacher and satirical novelist. *A Case of Samples,* 1962.

BROTHER ANTONINUS (William Everson), *American,* b. 1912. Dominican lay brother associated with San Francisco "Beat" movement in certain ways, but mostly a poetic disciple of Robinson Jeffers. *The Residual Years,* 1948; *The Crooked Lines of God,* 1959; *The Hazards of Holiness,* 1963.

JOHN BERRYMAN, *American,* b. 1914. University professor, critic, short-story writer, biographer. *The Dispossessed,* 1948; *Homage to Mistress Bradstreet,* 1959; *77 Dream Songs,* 1964.

JOHN BETJEMAN, *English,* b. 1906. Former schoolteacher; journalist, authority on British architecture. His *Collected Poems,* 1958, and *Summoned by Bells,* 1960, are the most popular books of verse published in England since World War II.

ELIZABETH BISHOP, *American,* b. 1911. For many years resident in Brazil. *North and South,* 1946; *Poems,* 1955; *Question of Travel,* 1965.

PAUL BLACKBURN, *American,* b. 1926. Editor, translator, associated with Black Mountain poets. *The Dissolving Fabric,* 1955.

THOMAS BLACKBURN, *English,* b. 1916. College lecturer, critic, anthologist. *The Next Word,* 1958; *A Smell of Burning,* 1961.

ROBERT BLY, *American,* b. 1926. Translator; editor, *The Sixties;* associated with Donald Hall, Louis Simpson, James Wright, and James Dickey in attempts to infuse a poetry of extreme simplicity with "surrealist" techniques borrowed from Lorca and other European models. *Silence in the Snowy Fields,* 1962.

EDWIN BROCK, *English,* b. 1927. Former policeman and trade journalist, now an advertising copywriter. *An Attempt at Exorcism,* 1959; *A Family Affair,* 1960; *With Love from Judas,* 1963.

HAYDEN CARRUTH, *American,* b. 1921. Critic, editor, novelist. *The Crow and the Hearth,* 1959; *The Norfolk Poems,* 1963; *Nothing for Tigers,* 1965.

CHARLES CAUSLEY, *English,* b. 1917. Schoolmaster, anthologist, broadcaster. *Farewell, Aggie Weston,* 1951; *Survivor's Leave,* 1953; *Union Street,* 1957; *Johnny Alleluia,* 1961.

JOHN CIARDI, *American*, b. 1916. University teacher, translator, poetry editor of the *Saturday Review*. *Other Skies*, 1947; *As If*, 1956; *I Marry You*, 1958; *39 Poems*, 1959; *In the Stoneworks*, 1961.

AUSTIN CLARKE, *Irish*, b. 1896. Dean of Irish poets, playwright, journalist; was younger associate of Yeats in Abbey Theatre. *Collected Poems*, 1935; *Later Poems*, 1961; *Flight to Africa*, 1963; *Mnemosyne Lay in Dust*, 1966.

ROBERT CONQUEST, *English*, b. 1917. Journalist, science fiction writer, expert on Soviet Union. Leading figure and anthologist of the "Movement," an attempt to shape a rationalist, anti-Romantic, anti-experimentalist poetry whose clarity, common sense, and wit would presumably express current British sensibility. *Poems*, 1955; *Between Mars and Venus*, 1962.

ROBERT CREELEY, *American*, b. 1926. University teacher, novelist, former editor of *Black Mountain Review*. *For Love: Poems 1950–1960*, 1962.

J. V. CUNNINGHAM, *American*, b. 1911. University professor, critic, advocate of a poetry of astringent restraint after the teachings of Yvor Winters. *The Exclusions of a Rhyme*, 1961.

DONALD DAVIE, *English*, b. 1922. Critic, university professor, translator. *Brides of Reason*, 1955; *A Winter Talent*, 1957; *New and Selected Poems*, 1961; *Events and Wisdoms*, 1964.

DENIS DEVLIN, *Irish*, 1908–1959. Diplomat, translator. *Selected Poems*, 1963, *Collected Poems*, 1964.

JAMES DICKEY, *American*, b. 1923. University teacher. *Unto the Stone*, 1960; *Drowning with Others*, 1962; *Buckdancer's Choice*, 1965.

ALAN DUGAN, *American*, b. 1923. Turned from work as handicraftsman (model-maker in plastics) to purely literary career after publication of first book. *Poems*, 1961; *Poems 2*, 1964.

ROBERT DUNCAN, *American*, b. 1919. Critic, editor, estheticist-mystic associated with Black Mountain group; experimenter with collage-like structures in longer works. *Letters*, 1958; *Selected Poems*, 1959; *The Opening of the Field*, 1960; *Roots and Branches*, 1964.

RICHARD EBERHART, *American*, b. 1904. Verse-playwright, professor (poet in residence). *Collected Poems*, 1960; *The Quarry*, 1964; *Selected Poems*, 1965.

D. J. ENRIGHT, *English*, b. 1920. University professor, critic, translator, anthologist, novelist; extensive experience in Far East. *The Laughing Hyena*, 1953; *Bread Rather than Blossoms*, 1956; *Some Men Are Brothers*, 1960; *Addictions*, 1962; *The Old Adam*, 1965.

LAWRENCE FERLINGHETTI, *American*, b. 1919. Publisher of City Lights Books, translator, an original participant in San Francisco "Beat" movement, contributing sophisticated notes related to the work of modern poets in France, where he studied for a doctorate. Now primarily a political satirist in his poetry and plays. *Pictures of the Gone World*, 1955; *A Coney Island of the Mind*, 1958; *Routines*, 1964.

IAN HAMILTON FINLAY, *Scottish*, b. 1925. Edinburgh poet, typographer and designer, associated with Concretist movement in poetry. Former road laborer, farm worker; publisher of Wild Hawthorn Press, editor of *Poor. Old. Tired. Horse*. *The Dancers Inherit the Party*, 1962; *Telegrams from My Windmill*, 1964.

DAVID GALLER, *American*, b. 1929. Trade magazine editor; production work in book publishing. *Walls and Distances*, 1959.

JACK GILBERT, *American*, b. 1925. Occasional university teacher, poet in residence. *Views of Jeopardy*, 1962.

ALLEN GINSBERG, *American*, b. 1926. Best-known, and probably most accomplished, of the "Beat" poets. *Howl*, 1956; *Empty Mirror*, 1960; *Kaddish*, 1960; *Reality Sandwiches*, 1963; *Jukebox All'ldregeno*, 1965.

PAUL GOODMAN, *American*, b. 1911. Outstanding nonconformist thinker and social critic; author of studies in city planning, *Gestalt* psychotherapy, esthetic theory, and adolescents' problems in the United States. Lay analyst. Novelist. *The Lordly Hudson*, 1962.

W. S. GRAHAM, *Scottish*, b. 1917. Employed by coast guard in Cornwall, where he lives in seclusion from literary world. *The Seven Journeys*, 1944; *Second Poems*, 1945; *The White Threshold*, 1949; *The Nightfishing*, 1955.

HORACE GREGORY, *American*, b. 1898. Translator of Catullus and Ovid; editor, critic, college teacher (retired). Was a leading poet of the thirties, but has done his most original work since the war. *Collected Poems*, 1964.

THOM GUNN, *English*, b. 1929. University teacher, critic, anthologist; has lived in California since 1954. *Fighting Terms*, 1954; *The Sense of Movement*, 1957; *My Sad Captains*, 1961.

RAMON GUTHRIE, *American*, b. 1896. Professor of French (retired), critic, translator. Member of the literary generation of the twenties and early thirties, in Paris and the United States, who re-emerged with *Graffiti*, 1959.

DONALD HALL, *American*, b. 1928. Professor, anthologist, critic; poetry editor for nine years of *Paris Review;* associated with "Sixties" group. *Exiles and Marriages*, 1955; *The Dark Houses*, 1958; *A Roof of Tiger Lilies*, 1964.

MICHAEL HAMBURGER, *British*, b. 1924. Born in Germany, came with family to Britain as refugees in 1933. University teacher; German scholar and translator, critic, short-story writer. *Flowering Cactus*, 1950; *Poems 1950–1951*, 1952; *The Dual Site*, 1958; *Weather and Season*, 1963.

ANTHONY HECHT, *American*, b. 1922. College teacher. *A Summoning of Stones*, 1954.

GEOFFREY HILL, *English*, b. 1932. University teacher. *For the Unfallen*, 1959.

JOHN HOLLOWAY, *English*, b. 1920. University teacher, anthologist, critic, *The Minute*, 1956; *The Fugue*, 1960; *The Landfallers*, 1962.

KATHERINE HOSKINS, *American*, b. 1909. *A Penitential Primer*, 1945; *Villa Narcisse*, 1956; *Out in the Open*, 1959.

GRAHAM HOUGH, *English*, b. 1908. Critic, professor, student of Romanticism. *Legends and Pastorals*, 1961.

TED HUGHES, *English*, b. 1930. The outstanding British poet of his generation. Short-story writer; radio and television dramatist. *The Hawk in the Rain*, 1957; *Lupercal*, 1960.

RANDALL JARRELL, *American*, 1914–1965. Professor, critic, translator, editor, novelist. *Selected Poems*, 1955; *The Woman at the Washington Zoo*, 1960; *The Lost World*, 1965.

ELIZABETH JENNINGS, *English*, b. 1926. Librarian, publisher's reader, anthologist. *Poems*, 1953; *A Way of Looking*, 1955; *A Sense of the World*, 1958; *Song for a Birth or a Death*, 1961; *Every Changing Shape*, 1961.

LEROI JONES, *American*, b. 1934. Editor of *Yugen*, critic, student of jazz, playwright. *Preface to a Twenty Volume Suicide Note*, 1960; *The Dead Lecturer*, 1964.

PATRICK KAVANAGH, *Irish*, b. 1905. Has earned a difficult livelihood through various means including small farming and journalism; in recent years associated with the group around *X* magazine, edited in London during its existence by David Wright. *Collected Poems,* 1964.

GALWAY KINNELL, *American,* b. 1927. Teacher, translator. *What a Kingdom It Was,* 1960; *Flower Herding on Mount Monadnock,* 1964.

THOMAS KINSELLA, *Irish,* b. 1928. Civil servant, Department of Finance; translator. Artist in residence, Southern Illinois University. *Another September,* 1958; *Poems and Translations,* 1961; *Downstream,* 1962; *Wormwood,* 1966.

CAROLYN KIZER, *American,* b. 1925. Editor, *Poetry Northwest;* teacher, translator; American poet in residence, Pakistan. *The Ungrateful Garden,* 1961; *Knock upon Silence,* 1965.

STANLEY KUNITZ, *American,* b. 1905. Former journalist; occasional college teacher; formerly associated with Poetry Center (Young Men's Hebrew Association, New York City). *Selected Poems 1928–1958,* 1958.

DILYS LAING, *American,* 1906–1960. Canadian by birth; maiden name, under which reputation first began to be made, Dilys Bennett. Associated with Dartmouth group of poets, including Richard Eberhart and Ramon Guthrie. Translator, novelist. *Birth Is Farewell,* 1944; *Walk through Two Landscapes,* 1950; *Poems from a Cage,* 1961.

PHILIP LARKIN, *English,* b. 1922. University librarian; a poetic spokesman of the literary generation of "angry young men"; novelist. *The North Ship,* 1945; *The Less Deceived,* 1955; *The Whitsun Weddings,* 1964.

IRVING LAYTON, *Canadian,* b. 1912. College teacher, associated with Black Mountain group in United States. *The Improved Binoculars,* 1956; *A Laughter in the Mind,* 1958; *A Red Carpet for the Sun,* 1959.

DENISE LEVERTOV, *American,* b. 1923. British-born; married the novelist Mitchell Goodman and settled in the United States in 1948. Associated with Black Mountain group. Editor, occasional college lecturer. *The Double Image,* 1946; *Here and Now,* 1957; *Overland to the Islands,* 1958; *With Eyes at the Backs of Our Heads,* 1960; *The Jacob's Ladder,* 1961; *O Taste and See,* 1964.

JOHN LOGAN, *American,* b. 1923. University professor. *Cycle for Mother Cabrini,* 1955; *Ghosts of the Heart,* 1960; *Spring of the Thief,* 1963.

ROBERT LOWELL, *American,* b. 1917. The outstanding American poet to emerge since World War II, and the chief influence on the "confessional" school. Has taught in various universities. Translator. *Land of Unlikeness,* 1944; *Lord Weary's Castle,* 1946; *The Mills of the Kavanaughs,* 1951; *Life Studies,* 1959; *Imitations,* 1961; *For the Union Dead,* 1964; *The Old Glory* (dramatic drama), 1965.

GEORGE MACBETH, *Scottish,* b. 1932. BBC talks producer. *The Broken Places,* 1963; *A Doomsday Book,* 1965.

NORMAN MACCAIG, *Scottish,* b. 1910. Edinburgh schoolmaster. *Riding Lights,* 1956; *The Sinai Sort,* 1957; *A Common Grace,* 1960; *A Round of Applause,* 1962; *Measures,* 1965.

HUGH MACDIARMID (Christopher Grieve), *Scottish,* b. 1892. The leading modern Scottish poet, rivaled only by Edwin Muir. A Scottish Nationalist and Communist, he opposed the Prime Minister in the general election of 1964, standing in the same constituency. Though his greatest work has been in Scots, a considerable body of his writing in English is not only distinguished but virtually unknown to American readers. *Collected Poems,* 1962.

JAY MACPHERSON, *Canadian,* b. 1931. British-born university teacher. *Nineteen Poems,* 1952; *O Earth, Return,* 1954; *The Boatman,* 1957.

(274)

W. S. MERWIN, *American*, b. 1927. Translator, editor, journalist, playwright. *A Mask for Janus*, 1952; *The Dancing Bears*, 1954; *Green with Beasts*, 1956; *The Drunk in the Furnace*, 1960.

CHRISTOPHER MIDDLETON, *English*, b. 1926. University lecturer in German; translator, short-story writer, critic, librettist. *Poems*, 1944; *Nocturne in Eden*, 1945; *Torse 3*, 1962; *Nonsequences*, 1965.

JOHN MONTAGUE, *Irish*, b. 1929. American-born, has divided his time between Ireland (Dublin and Ulster) and living abroad—France, Mexico, the United States. Film critic, journalist, occasional university teacher. *Forms of Exile*, 1958; *Poisoned Lands*, 1961.

EDWIN MUIR, *Scottish*, 1887–1958. One of the most truly *European* authors of modern British literature. After a youth of poverty in Scotland, explored socialist, Freudian, mystical, and religious thought. Editor, translator, critic; author of an outstanding autobiography; Director, British Institute in Prague and Rome after World War II. *Collected Poems 1921–1951*, 1952; *One Foot in Eden*, 1957; *Collected Poems*, 1965.

RICHARD MURPHY, *Irish*, b. 1927. After British education, returned to Galway, where, among other activities, rebuilt and handles the old-time hooker *Ave Maria* for tourists who wish to go sailing and fishing on it. *The Last Galway Hooker*, 1961; *Sailing to an Island*, 1963.

HOWARD NEMEROV, *American*, b. 1920. Novelist, critic, former co-editor *Furioso*, college teacher. *New and Selected Poems*, 1960; *The Next Room of the Dream*, 1962.

DESMOND O'GRADY, *Irish*, b. 1932(?) Occasional teacher, at present living in Italy; *Reilly*, 1961; *Separazioni*, 1965.

CHARLES OLSON, *American*, b. 1910. Leading theorist of Black Mountain group; his essay on "projective verse" attempts in a way to carry forward William Carlos Williams' conceptions of functional technique, or what Olson calls "composition by field." *The Distances*, 1960; *The Maximus Poems*, 1960.

SYLVIA PLATH, *American*, 1932–1963. Wife of the British poet Ted Hughes; her suicidally intense last poems made an extraordinary impact after her death. *The Colossus*, 1962; *Ariel*, 1965.

PETER PORTER, *British*, b. 1929. Australian by birth. Associated with Peter Redgrove and others in "The Group," poets linked far more by their practice of meeting and criticizing one another's work than by strongly differentiated tenets (though at first they laid a certain emphasis on "healthy-minded" writing and on unadventurous technique). *Once Bitten, Twice Bitten*, 1961; *Poems Ancient and Modern*, 1964.

HENRY RAGO, *American*, b. 1915. Editor of *Poetry* magazine since 1955; trained in law and philosophy. *The Travelers*, 1949; *A Sky of Late Summer*, 1963.

PETER REDGROVE, *English*, b. 1932. Trained as a scientist, has turned to poetry and teaching. The most vigorous and idiosyncratic poet by far of those associated with "The Group." *The Collector*, 1959; *The Nature of Cold Weather*, 1961; *At the White Monument*, 1963.

KENNETH REXROTH, *American*, b. 1905. Journalist, critic, translator, associated with various avant-garde movements and West Coast political nonconformism. *In Defense of the Earth*, 1956; *Natural Numbers*, 1963.

ANNE RIDLER, *English*, b. 1912. Editor, critic, verse-playwright. *Selected Poems*, 1961.

W. R. RODGERS, *Irish*, b. 1909. An Ulsterman, for twelve years a Presbyterian clergyman in Armagh. Producer, British Broadcasting Corporation, 1946–1952. *Awake!*, 1941; *Europa and the Bull*, 1952.

THEODORE ROETHKE, *American*, 1908–1963. University professor; in his later years a central figure among poets of the Pacific Northwest while his national and international reputation was rapidly growing. *Words for the Wind*, 1958; *The Far Field*, 1964.

JEROME ROTHENBERG, *American*, b. 1932. Translator, editor. *The Seven Hells of Jigoku Zoshi*, 1960.

MURIEL RUKEYSER, *American*, b. 1913. College teacher, critic, biographer, translator, cultural historian with a special interest in correlations between scientific theory and esthetic principles. *Waterlily Fire*, 1963.

JAMES SCHEVILL, *American*, b. 1920. College professor, Director of Poetry Center (San Francisco State College), playwright, editor, biographer. *Public Dooms and Private Destinations*, 1963; *The Stalingrad Elegies*, 1964.

DELMORE SCHWARTZ, *American*, 1913–1966. Editor, college teacher, verse-playwright. *Summer Knowledge*, 1959.

WINFIELD TOWNLEY SCOTT, *American*, b. 1910. Critic, former literary editor of *Providence Journal*. *Collected Poems*, 1962.

ANNE SEXTON, *American*, b. 1928. Once for a short time a fashion model; disciple of "confessional" poetic school of Robert Lowell and W. D. Snodgrass. *Selected Poems*, 1964.

KARL SHAPIRO, *American*, b. 1913. Former editor, *Poetry* magazine and then *Prairie Schooner*. University professor, critic, who in recent years has tried to lead a revolt against the Pound-Eliot influence, the influence of criticism, and the assumptions of academic discipline in the study of literature. *Poems*, 1953; *Poems of a Jew*, 1958; *The Bourgeois Poet*, 1964.

JON SILKIN, *English*, b. 1930. Editor, teacher, critic. *The Peaceable Kingdom*, 1954; *The Two Freedoms*, 1958; *The Re-Ordering of the Stones*, 1961.

LOUIS SIMPSON, *American*, b. 1923. Professor, critic, fiction writer, associated with "Sixties" group. *Good News of Death*, 1955; *A Dream of Governors*, 1959; *At the End of the Open Road*, 1963.

ROBIN SKELTON, *Irish*, b. 1925. University lecturer, editor, anthologist, critic, literary historian. *The Dark Window*, 1962.

A. J. M. SMITH, *American*, b. 1902. Canadian-born university professor, critic, anthologist, student of Canadian literature, translator. *Collected Poems*, 1963.

W. D. SNODGRASS, *American*, b. 1926. University teacher, translator. *Heart's Needle*, 1959, is especially in the title poem an outstanding example of postwar "confessional" poetry.

GARY SNYDER, *American*, b. 1930. Has worked at sea and in West Coast logging jobs; residence in Japan for a number of years. *Riprap*, 1959; *Myths and Texts*, 1960; *A Range of Poems*, 1966.

WILLIAM STAFFORD, *American*, b. 1914. College professor. *West of Your City*, 1960; *Traveling Through the Dark*, 1962.

GEORGE STARBUCK, *American*, b. 1931. Editor. *Bone Thoughts*, 1960.

MAY SWENSON, *American*, b. 1919. *Another Animal*, 1954 (in *Poets of Today: I*); *A Cage of Spines*, 1958; *To Mix with Time*, 1963.

R. S. THOMAS, *Welsh*, b. 1913. Welsh priest (vicar of Eglwys Fach); anthologist. *Stones of the Field*, 1947; *Poetry for Supper*, 1958; *Tares*, 1961; *The Bread of Truth*, 1963.

ANTHONY THWAITE, *English*, b. 1930. BBC producer; former literary editor, *The Listener. Home Truths*, 1962; *The Owl in the Trees*, 1963.

CHARLES TOMLINSON, *English*, b. 1927. University teacher, strongly influenced by American poetry. *Relations and Contraries*, 1951; *The Necklace*, 1955; *Seeing Is Believing*, 1958; *A Peopled Landscape*, 1963; *American Scenes*, 1966.

JOHN WAIN, *English*, b. 1925. University teacher, critic, journalist, novelist. *A Word Curved as a Sill*, 1956; *Weep before God*, 1961; *Hidden Life*, 1962; *Wildtrack*, 1965.

RICHARD WEBER, *Irish*, b. 1932. Editor, assistant librarian. *The Time Being*, 1957; *Lady and Gentleman*, 1963.

THEODORE WEISS, *American*, b. 1916. College professor; editor, with Renée Weiss, of *Quarterly Review of Literature. The Catch*, 1951; *Outlanders*, 1960; *Gunsight*, 1964; *The Medium*, 1965.

REED WHITTEMORE, *American*, b. 1919. College professor; editor, *Furioso* and now *Carleton Miscellany. Heroes and Heroines*, 1946; *An American Takes a Walk*, 1956; *The Self-Made Man*, 1959; *The Boy from Iowa*, 1962.

RICHARD WILBUR, *American*, b. 1921. College professor, translator. *The Beautiful Changes*, 1947; *Ceremony*, 1950; *Things of This World*, 1956; *Advice to a Prophet*, 1961.

DAVID WRIGHT, *British*, b. 1920. Born in South Africa; edited *X* magazine; translator, anthologist, critic, free-lance writer. *Monologue of a Deaf Man*, 1958; *Adam at Evening*, 1965.

JAMES WRIGHT, *American*, b. 1927. University teacher, member of "Sixties" group. *The Green Wall*, 1957; *Saint Judas*, 1959; *The Branch Will Not Break*, 1963.

MARYA ZATURENSKA, *American*, b. 1902. Russian-born wife of Horace Gregory; critic, anthologist, literary historian. *Collected Poems*, 1965.

Index of Authors and Titles

(2 7 9)

(2 8 1)

(2 8 3)